Englisch
Gebrauch der Zeiten
5./6. Klasse

D1694560

Barbara E. Oehl, B. A., P. G. C. E.

© 1999 Compact Verlag München
Redaktion: Alexandra Dietrich, Dietmar Hefendehl
Redaktionsassistenz: Melinda Csáky, Alparslan Bayramli
Umschlaggestaltung: Gesche Harms
Illustrationen: Gesche Harms
Produktionsleitung: Uwe Eckhard

ISBN 3-8174-7081-9
7370811

Besuchen Sie uns im Internet www.compactverlag.de!

Inhalt

Völlig zeitlos?

Stell dir vor, es gäbe eine Sprache, in der du dich nur über die Gegenwart unterhalten kannst. Nie kannst du erzählen, was du in der Vergangenheit gemacht hast, oder was du in der Zukunft noch machen willst.

Damit wärst du ganz schön eingeschränkt in deinem Sprachgebrauch. Du könntest noch nicht mal erfragen, was dein Freund oder deine Freundin gestern gemacht hat und für morgen verabreden könntet ihr euch auch nicht!

Wenn du dich über die Vergangenheit und die Zukunft unterhalten willst, dann brauchst du dafür verschiedene Zeitformen. Und du benötigst Informationen darüber, wie sie gebildet, verwendet und kombiniert werden können. Sonst sagst du am Ende noch Sachen wie "Ich werde gestern einkaufen gehen", oder gar "Ich wirst einkaufen geht." Die Folge ist dann, dass keiner genau weiß, was du eigentlich sagen wolltest. Im Englischen ist das ganz genauso!

Es ist also wirklich wichtig, dass du weißt, wie du im Englischen die verschiedenen Zeiten bildest und es ist ebenso wichtig, dass du weißt, was du damit anfangen kannst.

Dass dies gar nicht so schwer ist, zeigt dir dieses Buch:

1. Zu jedem Thema, das ihr in der 5. und 6. Klasse behandelt, findest du hier eine Doppelseite. Links sind immer die Erklärungen und die Beispiele, damit du alles verstehst. Rechts kannst du dann selbst üben, wie du die Verbformen bildest und wie du sie anwendest. So kannst du dir sicher schon bald alles gut merken. Eine Doppelseite kannst du in 45 Minuten schaffen. Die Übungen fangen ganz leicht an und werden langsam schwieriger. Du solltest immer eine Doppelseite an einem Übungstag bearbeiten.

2. Wir empfehlen dir, ein Extra-Heft zu besorgen, in das du deine Übungen schreibst. Es kann nämlich vorkommen, dass du für manche Aufgaben im Buch nicht genügend Platz findest. Diese Übungen erkennst du an dem Symbol mit dem **Bleistift** und dem **Blatt Papier**.

3. Wichtige Regeln und Merksätze sind am Rand mit einem **dicken Zeigefinger** oder einem **Ausrufezeichen** markiert.
An den Stellen, an denen du besonders aufpassen musst, findest du eine **offene Hand** oder eine **Glühbirne**.

4. Lerntipps, die mit einem **Tipp-Symbol** gekennzeichnet sind, helfen dir, immer wieder das Lernen zu lernen.

5. Eine **Lesebrille** am Rand kennzeichnet die Beispiele, mit denen dir die jeweiligen Regeln veranschaulicht werden.

6. Aufgaben, bei denen du aufgefordert wirst, etwas zu tun, sind mit einem **Zeigefingerbleistift** markiert.
Nur der **Bleistift** weist darauf hin, dass du bei folgender Aufgabe etwas einsetzen, ankreuzen oder verbinden sollst.
Bei schwierigen Aufgaben, bei denen du etwas mehr nachdenken oder selber einmal einen Satz schreiben musst, findest du einen **Wecker** oder einen **Daumen**, der **nach oben zeigt**.
Die **Trillerpfeife** sagt dir, dass es jetzt in den Endspurt geht.

7. Wenn du eine Aufgabe gelöst hast, dann kannst du im **Lösungsteil** ganz hinten im Buch nachschauen, ob du alles richtig gemacht hast. Das ist wichtig, damit du dir nichts Falsches merkst!

Und nun wünscht dir dein Power Pauker viel Spaß und Erfolg beim Lernen!

Gegenwart

to be: am / are / is

I am happy.

Hi, my name **is** Tom.
I'm a pupil. I**'m** 10 years old. I **am** from Ballynure. I**'m** interested in computers.
My parents **are** astronauts.

This **is** my sister.
Her name **is** Lisa.

And this **is** our dog,
Blacky.

Bejahte Form (also die Form *ohne* nicht):

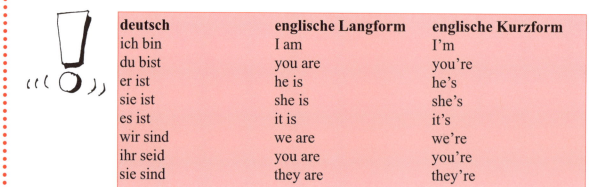

deutsch	englische Langform	englische Kurzform
ich bin	I am	I'm
du bist	you are	you're
er ist	he is	he's
sie ist	she is	she's
es ist	it is	it's
wir sind	we are	we're
ihr seid	you are	you're
sie sind	they are	they're

Im Englischen brauchst du die Langform, wenn du Aufsätze oder gar formale Briefe, z. B. an die Königin, schreibst.
Beim Reden und für Briefe an Freunde und Verwandte kannst du gerne die Kurzform verwenden.

1. Wie viele der Sätze kannst du richtig sortieren?

1. a baker / My father / is / .
   _____

2. a planet / is / Jupiter/ .
   _____

3. are / noisy / The pupils / .
   _____

4. Apples / are / bananas / and / types of fruit / .
   _____

5. York / London / in England / cities / and / are / .
   _____

2. Vervollständige diese Sätze mit *am* oder *is* oder *are*:

1. My brother _____ a taxi driver.
2. Nils and Lars _____ German.
3. I _____ 12 years old.
4. Richard and I _____ friends.
5. You _____ a good tennis player.

3. Wie kannst du die folgenden Sätze auf Englisch sagen?
Diese Wörter helfen dir dabei: boring tired fantastic hungry tall

1. Wir sind hungrig.
   _____

2. Ich bin groß.
   _____

3. Sie sind langweilig.
   _____

4. Das ist phantastisch!
   _____

5. Du bist müde.
   _____

He isn't hungry.

Hi, my name **isn't** Samantha.
I**'m not** a teacher.
I**'m not** from the South Pole.
My parents **aren't** doctors.

And this **isn't** our cat.

This **isn't** my sister.

Verneinte Form (also die Form *mit* nicht):

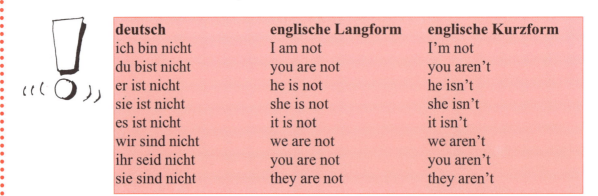

deutsch	englische Langform	englische Kurzform
ich bin nicht	I am not	I'm not
du bist nicht	you are not	you aren't
er ist nicht	he is not	he isn't
sie ist nicht	she is not	she isn't
es ist nicht	it is not	it isn't
wir sind nicht	we are not	we aren't
ihr seid nicht	you are not	you aren't
sie sind nicht	they are not	they aren't

4. Was gehört in die Lücke: *'m not* oder *isn't* oder *aren't*?

1. You _____ stupid. You are clever.
2. Mr. Bean _____ a policeman. He is a comedian.
3. We _____ hungry. We are thirsty.
4. I _____ a teacher. I'm a pupil.
5. Tom and Jerry _____ dogs. Tom is a cat and Jerry is a mouse.

5. Behaupte jeweils das Gegenteil!
Beispiel: *He is silly.* ➔ *He isn't silly.*

1. This chair is comfortable.
This chair _____ comfortable.
2. I am old.
I _____ old.
3. This CD is cheap.
This CD _____ cheap.
4. These exercises are difficult.
These exercises _____ difficult.
5. This car is yellow.
This car _____ yellow.

6. Wie kannst du die folgenden Sätze auf Englisch sagen?
Diese Wörter helfen dir dabei: thirsty untidy expensive happy short

1. Diese Schuhe sind nicht teuer.

_____

2. Lawrence ist nicht klein.

_____

3. Wir sind nicht glücklich.

_____

4. Er ist nicht unordentlich.

_____

5. Ich bin nicht durstig.

_____

Are you tired?

to be – Frageform und Kurzantwort:

deutsche Frage	englische Frage	Kurzantwort
bin ich ?	am I ?	Yes, I am. / No, I'm not.
bist du ?	are you ?	Yes, you are. / No, you aren't.
ist er ?	is he ?	Yes, he is. / No, he isn't.
ist sie ?	is she ?	Yes, she is. / No, she isn't.
ist es ?	is it ?	Yes, it is. / No, it isn't.
sind wir ?	are we ?	Yes, we are. / No, we aren't.
seid ihr ?	are you ?	Yes, you are. / No, you aren't.
sind sie ?	are they ?	Yes, they are. / No, they aren't.

Fragen mit Fragewörtern, zum Beispiel *what*, *where*, *why*:

What .... ? (*Was? / Welche?*)

Where ....? (*Wo?*)

Why ....? (*Warum?*)

What **is** your problem?
What colour **are** your shoes?
Where **are** you?
Where **is** your sister?
Why **are** you tired?
Why **is** he angry?

7. Welche Form von *am* oder *is* oder *are* gehört in die erste Lücke und welche Kurzantwort in die zweite?

Denk daran, dass immer das erste Wort in einer Frage mit einem Großbuchstaben anfängt.

1. _____ Garfield a dog?
   No, he _____ .
2. _____ I late?
   Yes, you _____.
3. _____ you the President of the United States of America?
   No, I _____.
4. _____ this your bicycle?
   Yes, it _____ .
5. _____ they at home?
   No, they _____ .

8. Wie kannst du die folgenden Sätze auf Englisch sagen?
Diese Wörter helfen dir dabei:
children angry a doctor crazy in bed ready

1. Sind wir fertig?
   _____
2. Ist sie (eine) Ärztin?
   _____
3. Sind die Kinder im Bett?
   _____
4. Bist du ärgerlich?
   _____
5. Seid ihr verrückt?
   _____

9. Bilde nun Fragen mit Fragewörtern.
Benutze die folgenden Wörter: what where so quiet who why wrong

1. Wo ist das?   _____
2. Wer sind sie?   _____
3. Was ist falsch?   _____
4. Warum bist du so still? _____
5. Wie heißt du?   _____

11

present progressive

Wenn du ausdrücken möchtest, dass etwas jetzt gerade passiert, dann brauchst du im **Deutschen** meistens zusätzliche Wörter.
Du kannst dann zum Beispiel sagen: *Er telefoniert gerade.*
oder: *Er ist gerade dabei zu telefonieren.*

Wenn du im **Englischen** ausdrücken möchtest, dass etwas jetzt gerade passiert, dann brauchst du keine zusätzlichen Wörter, sondern nur eine bestimmte Verbform, das sogenannte **present progressive** in der bejahten Form. Manchmal sagen deine Lehrerinnen oder Lehrer vielleicht auch *present continuous* dazu – damit ist aber das Gleiche gemeint.

We are dancing in the rain.

He is eating an ice-cream.

present progressive – bejahte Form:

deutsch	englische Langform	englische Kurzform
ich esse gerade	I am eating	I'm eating
du isst gerade	you are eating	you're eating
er isst gerade	he is eating	he's eating
sie isst gerade	she is eating	she's eating
es isst gerade	it is eating	it's eating
wir essen gerade	we are eating	we're eating
ihr esst gerade	you are eating	you're eating
sie essen gerade	they are eating	they're eating

10. Welche der Lücken kannst du richtig füllen? Bei welchen weißt du, ob *am*, *is* oder *are* hingehört? Benutze jeweils eine dieser **„ing-Formen"**!
Diese Wörter helfen dir dabei: playing   wearing   going   trying   waiting

1. "Look! Jason _____ a funny hat."
2. "Hurry up! I _____ for you."
3. "Listen! Andrew _____ the piano."
4. "What are you doing?" – "I _____ to
   open this box."
5. "Where are you going now ?" – "We _____ to the museum."

I am watching TV.

11. Übersetze! Bilde die richtige *ing*-Form mit diesen Wörtern:
to listen to   to have breakfast   new trousers   the trumpet   to land
to wear   to rain   to climb a tree   a newspaper   to visit   to bark
to read

1. Die Katze klettert (gerade) auf einen Baum.

   _____

2. Hör mal! Die Hunde bellen (gerade).

   _____

3. Moritz besucht (gerade) einen Freund.

   _____

4. Wir frühstücken (gerade).

   _____

5. Das Flugzeug landet (gerade).

   _____

6. Es regnet (gerade).

   _____

7. Schau mal! Claudia hat ihre neue Hose (gerade) an.

   _____

8. Hör mal! Raymond spielt (gerade) Trompete.

   _____

9. Papa liest (gerade) Zeitung.

   _____

10. Mama hört (gerade) Musik.

    _____

ing-Form

Wie du schon gesehen hast, brauchst du die **ing**-Form, um diese Zeit bilden zu können. Wenn in deinem Grammatikbuch *Verlaufsform* oder *Partizip Präsens* oder *present participle* steht, dann ist genau das damit gemeint: die ing-Form.

Bei den meisten Wörtern ist es sehr leicht, die ing-Form zu bilden. Du hängst einfach hinten an die **Grundfom des englischen Verbes -ing** an, z. B. *to go* → *going*

Pass auf, dass du die ing-Form immer richtig schreibst:

→ **stummes *-e* am Ende fällt weg.** Beispiel: to take + -ing → taking
→ ***-ie* am Ende wird zu *-y*.** Beispiel: to lie + -ing → lying
→ ***-el* am Ende wird verdoppelt.** Beispiel: to travel + -ing → travelling

Bei der Bildung der ing-Form wird außerdem **der letzte Konsonant verdoppelt**, wenn

✓ der **vorletzte** Buchstabe des Infinitivs (nicht der letzte!) **ein** Vokal (nicht zwei oder drei Vokale!) ist **und**
✓ der **letzte** (nicht der vorletzte!) **ein** Konsonant, (nicht mehrere!) **und**
✓ die letzte Silbe des Wortes **betont** (nicht unbetont!) ist.

Beispiel: to begin + -ing → beginning

Regelmäßig gebildet werden aber zum Beispiel Wörter, die 2 Konsonanten am Ende haben:
to climb + -ing → climbing,
bei denen 2 Vokale vor dem Konsonanten stehen:
to meet + -ing → meeting,
deren letzte Silbe unbetont ist:
to kayak + -ing → kayaking.

Wörter, die auf *-y* oder *-w* enden, werden ebenfalls regelmäßig gebildet:
trying, staying, growing, showing usw.

12. Bilde die ing-Form dieser Verben und achte dabei auf die richtige Schreibweise:

1. to write

_____

2. to swim

_____

3. to listen

_____

4. to run

_____

5. to drive

_____

6. to wear

_____

7. to help

_____

8. to get

_____

9. to look

_____

10. to have

_____

11. to open

_____

12. to stop

_____

The sun isn't shining.

Wenn du im Englischen ausdrücken möchtest, dass etwas jetzt gerade **nicht** passiert, dann brauchst du keine zusätzlichen Wörter, sondern nur eine bestimmte Verbform, das **present progressive in der verneinten Form**, das sogenannte **present progressive negative**.

It is raining.
The sun **isn't** shining.

We are watching TV.
We **aren't** listening to the radio.
We **aren't** reading a newspaper.

present progressive – verneinte Form:

englische Langform	englische Kurzform
I am not working	I'm not working
you are not working	you aren't working
he is not working	he isn't working
she is not working	she isn't working
it is not working	it isn't working
we are not working	we aren't working
you are not working	you aren't working
they are not working	they aren't working

13. Was gehört in die Lücke: **'m not**, **isn't** oder **aren't**?

1. Dermot _____ laughing. He is crying.
2. We _____ having breakfast. We are having lunch.
3. Sinead _____ feeling okay. She has got a temperature.
4. I _____ walking to the disco. I am going by bus.
5. Paula and Steve _____ flying to Dublin. They are flying to Belfast.

14. Behaupte jeweils das Gegenteil!
Beispiel: We **are reading** a newspaper.
→ We **aren't reading** a newspaper.

1. I am eating an apple.
   I _____ an apple.
2. We are having dinner.
   We _____ dinner.
3. It is snowing.
   It _____ .
4. They are writing postcards.
   They _____ postcards.
5. The phone is ringing.
   The phone _____ .

15. Wie kannst du die folgenden Sätze auf Englisch sagen? Denk daran, dass du hier das Wort **keinen** durch **nicht einen** ersetzen kannst.
Diese Wörter können dir helfen: his homework   a hat   in the garden   an elephant   to me

1. Die Kinder spielen (jetzt) nicht im Garten.

_____

2. Ich trage (jetzt) keinen Hut.

_____

3. Du hörst mir (gerade) nicht zu!

_____

4. Christopher macht (jetzt) nicht seine Hausaufgaben.

_____

5. Ich reite (gerade) keinen Elefanten.

_____

Are you going to a party?

What are they talking about?

present progressive – Frageform und Kurzantwort:

englische Frage	Kurzantwort
am I watching?	Yes, I am. / No, I'm not.
are you watching?	Yes, you are. / No, you aren't.
is he watching?	Yes, he is. / No, he isn't.
is she watching?	Yes, she is. / No, she isn't.
is it watching?	Yes, it is. / No, it isn't.
are we watching?	Yes, we are. / No, we aren't.
are you watching?	Yes, you are. / No, you aren't.
are they watching?	Yes, they are. / No, they aren't.

Fragen mit Fragewörtern:

What .... ? (*Was? / Welche?*)   What **is** Raymond eat**ing**?
                                          What **are** you do**ing**?

Where ....? (*Wo? / Wohin?*)   Where **are** we go**ing**?
                                          Where **is** your brother stay**ing**?

Why ....? (*Warum?*)   Why **are** you laugh**ing**?
                                          Why **is** she shout**ing**?

How ....? (*Wie?*)   How **are** you feel**ing**?
                                          How **is** it go**ing**?

16. Welche Form von **to be** gehört in die erste Lücke, welche Kurzantwort gehört in die zweite Lücke?

1. _____ they having breakfast?   Yes, they _____ .
2. _____ he listening?   No, he _____ .
3. _____ you having a wash?   Yes, I _____ .
4. _____ we going to the party?   No, we _____ .
5. _____ she walking to school today?   Yes, she _____ .

17. Wie kannst du die folgenden Fragen im Englischen stellen?
Verwende folgende Wörter: to repair   to make tea   to have a shower zoo   to have lunch

1. Esst ihr (gerade) zu Mittag?

_____

2. Duschst du (gerade)?

_____

3. Repariert sie (gerade) ihr Fahrrad?

_____

4. Machst du (gerade) Tee?

_____

5. Geht ihr (gerade) in den Zoo?

_____

18. Benutze nun Fragewörter und bilde damit Fragen in der **Verlaufsform**.
Diese Wörter helfen dir: to tidy up   to leave   to cry   to go   to say

1. Wohin gehst du?

_____

2. Was sagen sie?

_____

3. Wer räumt auf?

_____

4. Warum weinst du?

_____

5. Wann gehst du weg?

_____

present simple

Wenn du auf Englisch ausdrücken möchtest, dass
• etwas regelmäßig passiert oder
• etwas immer gültig ist,
dann brauchst du eine andere Verbform, das sogenannte **present simple in der bejahten Form**.

Um die Regelmäßigkeit oder die Häufigkeit genauer auszudrücken, verwendet man dann in so einem Satz häufig noch die sogenannten **Häufigkeitsadverbien**, wie zum Beispiel:
✓ *often* (oft)
✓ *never* (niemals)
✓ *always* (immer)
✓ *usually* (gewöhnlich)
✓ *sometimes* (manchmal)
So ein **Häufigkeitsadverb** steht an einer anderen Stelle als im deutschen Satz. Im Englischen kommt es **vor** das Vollverb!
Beispiel: *Es regnet **oft**.*
             *It **often** rains.*

We often go to Ballyclare.

present simple – bejahte Form:

deutsch	englisch
ich mag	I like
du magst	you like
er mag	he likes
sie mag	she likes
es mag	it likes
wir mögen	we like
ihr mögt	you like
sie mögen	they like

19. Fülle die Lücken aus!

Denk bei *he*, *she* oder *it* immer an das *-s*!

Diese Wörter kannst du einsetzen: to speak   to work   to like   to open
to read

1. I _____ a lot of books.
2. The shops _____ at 9 o'clock.
3. Mr. Fisher _____ big cities.
4. We _____ very hard.
5. She _____ German, English, French and Swedish.

He never **eats** fish.

20. Welche der Sätze kannst du richtig sortieren? Erinnere dich daran, dass
das *Häufigkeitsadverb* im Englischen **vor** dem Vollverb steht!

1. rings / **often** / The phone / .

_____

2. work / **always** / from 9 to 5 / We / .

_____

3. gets / up / **never** / before / 6 o'clock / She / .

_____

4. does / **usually** / He / his homework / .

_____

5. play / **sometimes** / the guitar / I / .

_____

21. Wie kannst du die Sätze auf Englisch sagen? Pass wieder gut auf, damit
du die Häufigkeitsadverbien an die richtige Stelle im Satz schreibst!

1. Wir stehen **gewöhnlich** um 7 Uhr auf.   _____
2. Er macht **immer** seine Hausaufgaben.   _____
3. Ich gehe **manchmal** ins Kino.   _____
4. Sie gehen **oft** mit ihrem Hund raus.   _____
5. Du hörst mir **nie** zu!   _____

he, she, it – *s* muss mit!

Für die Gegenwartsform für **he**, **she** oder **it** gibt es **Regeln**, die dir helfen, diese Verbformen richtig zu schreiben.
- Die meisten Verben hängen an den **Infinitiv** ein -*s* an.

Aber:
- Sind die **letzten Buchstaben -*ss*, -*sh*, -*ch*** oder **-*x***, dann wird **-*es*** angehängt.
  Beispiel für -*ss*:   to discu**ss** →   he discu**sses**
  Beispiel für -*sh*:   to cra**sh**   →   he cra**shes**
  Beispiel für -*ch*:   to fet**ch**   →   he fet**ches**
  Beispiel für -*x*:   to fi**x**   →   he fi**xes**

He never catches any mice, but he always fetches the newspaper.

- Verben, die auf **Konsonant + -*y*** enden, hängen dann **-*ies*** an.
  Beispiel für **Konsonant + -*y*:**   to **try** →   he **tries**

- Verben, die auf **Vokal + -*y*** enden, hängen nur **-*s*** an.
  Beispiel für **Vokal + -*y*:**   to ob**ey** →   he ob**eys**

22. Wie lautet die richtige Form für **he**, **she** oder **it** im **simple present**?
Achte dabei gut auf die Schreibweise!

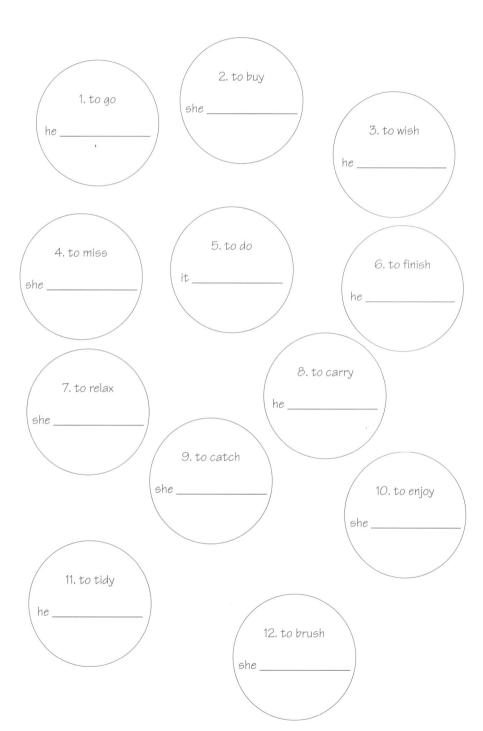

1. to go

he _____

2. to buy

she _____

3. to wish

he _____

4. to miss

she _____

5. to do

it _____

6. to finish

he _____

7. to relax

she _____

8. to carry

he _____

9. to catch

she _____

10. to enjoy

she _____

11. to tidy

he _____

12. to brush

she _____

He doesn't read a lot.

Wenn du im Englischen ausdrücken möchtest, dass
- etwas regelmäßig nicht passiert,
- etwas nicht gültig ist,

dann brauchst du auch das sogennante **present simple**, aber **in der verneinten Form**.

Für solche verneinten Sätze im **present simple** brauchst du die
richtige Form von   to do + not + Infinitiv

Beispiel: He   does   not   drink coffee. (Er trinkt keinen Kaffee.)
              We   do   not   drink coffee. (Wir trinken keinen
                                               Kaffee.)

present simple – verneinte Form:

deutsch	englische Langform	englische Kurzform
ich spiele nicht	I do not play	I don't play
du spielst nicht	you do not play	you don't play
er spielt nicht	he **does** not play	he doesn't play
sie spielt nicht	she **does** not play	she doesn't play
es spielt nicht	it d**oes** not play	it doesn't play
wir spielen nicht	we do not play	we don't play
ihr spielt nicht	you do not play	you don't play
sie spielen nicht	they do not play	they don't play

Wie du siehst, wird nur bei **he, she** und **it** ein **-es** an das **do angehängt**.
Sonst wird kein einziges **-s** mehr angehängt!

23. Was gehört in die Lücke: *don't* oder *doesn't*?

1. They _____ like sausages. They like chocolate.
2. Bill _____ play the piano. He plays the saxophone.
3. I _____ see him very often.
4. Katrina _____ collect stamps. She collects CDs.
5. We _____ want to do our homework. It is boring.

24. Behaupte jeweils das Gegenteil!
   Beispiele: We **read** books. → We **don't read** books.
   aber: He **reads** books. → He **doesn't read** books.

1. I eat meat.
   I _____ meat.
2. He plays the trumpet.
   He _____ the trumpet.
3. She likes classical music.
   She _____ classical music.
4. They like horror films.
   They _____ horror films.
5. He has a budgie.
   He _____ a budgie.

25. Wie kannst du die folgenden Sätze auf Englisch sagen?

Denk daran, dass du manchmal die Form **doesn't** und manchmal die Form **don't** brauchst!

Hier sind einige hilfreiche Wörter: dancing   on Saturdays   the piano
English   a car

1. Ich habe kein Auto.   _____
2. Wir arbeiten samstags nicht.   _____
3. Sharon spielt nicht Klavier.   _____
4. Jonathan geht nicht Tanzen.   _____
5. Sie sprechen nicht Englisch.   _____

25

Do you like horror films?

present simple – Frageform und Kurzantwort:

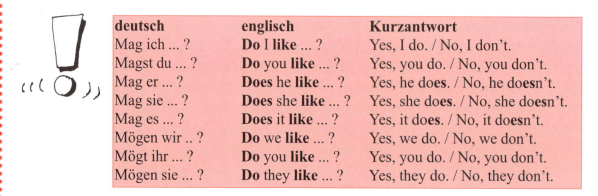

deutsch	englisch	Kurzantwort
Mag ich ... ?	**Do** I **like** ... ?	Yes, I do. / No, I don't.
Magst du ... ?	**Do** you **like** ... ?	Yes, you do. / No, you don't.
Mag er ... ?	**Does** he **like** ... ?	Yes, he does. / No, he doesn't.
Mag sie ... ?	**Does** she **like** ... ?	Yes, she does. / No, she doesn't.
Mag es ... ?	**Does** it **like** ... ?	Yes, it does. / No, it doesn't.
Mögen wir .. ?	**Do** we **like** ... ?	Yes, we do. / No, we don't.
Mögt ihr ... ?	**Do** you **like** ... ?	Yes, you do. / No, you don't.
Mögen sie ... ?	**Do** they **like** ... ?	Yes, they do. / No, they don't.

26. Welche Form von **to do** gehört in die erste Lücke und welche in die zweite?
Denk daran, immer das erste Wort einer Frage mit einem Großbuchstaben zu schreiben.

1. _____ they live in a small village?
Yes, they _____ .

2. _____ he drink a lot of coffee?
No, he _____ .

3. _____ you know the answer?
Yes, I _____ .

4. _____ we have a lot of work to do?
No, we _____ .

5. _____ she have a lot of money?
Yes, she _____ .

27. Welche Fragen kannst du nun selbst ins Englische übersetzen?
Diese Wörter helfen dir dabei: hamster   chocolate   to go on holiday
to speak   football

1. Fahrt ihr oft in Urlaub? _____
2. Hast du einen Hamster? _____
3. Spielen sie Fußball? _____
4. Sprechen sie Deutsch? _____
5. Mögt ihr Schokolade? _____

28. Bilde nun Fragen mit Fragewörtern.
Diese Verben sollen dir dabei helfen: to look   to go to the cinema
to mean   to live   to get up

1. Wo wohnst du?
_____

2. Was bedeutet das?
_____

3. Wie sieht es aus?
_____

4. Wie oft gehst du ins Kino?
_____

5. Wann steht ihr (immer) auf?
_____

Keine Verlaufsform!

Nicht alle Verben sind gleich. Die meisten Verben beschreiben Tätigkeiten oder Vorgänge, z. B: *to walk, to read, to rain.* Diese Verben haben eine einfache Form und eine Verlaufsform.

Es gibt aber nicht nur Tätigkeiten oder Vorgänge, die gerade passieren können. Es gibt auch **Zustände** oder **Standpunkte**, und die **können nicht gerade passieren**. Du würdest im Deutschen auch nicht sagen, dass du gerade dabei bist, etwas zu haben (1) oder dass du gerade dabei bist, etwas zu wissen (2) oder dass du gerade dabei bist, etwas zu mögen. (3)

Now I understand!

Hier die wichtigsten Verben, die üblicherweise NICHT in der Verlaufsform verwendet werden:

(1) Verben, die ausdrücken, was jemand **ist** oder was er **besitzt**, usw.:
be   have (*besitzen*)

(2) Verben, die ausdrücken, was man **weiß**, **versteht**, **denkt**, usw.:
think   mean   understand
remember   know

(3) Verben, die ausdrücken, was man **mag**, **nicht mag**, **wünscht**, usw.:
like   love   need
hate   want

Auch Verben der **Sinneswahrnehmung** haben üblicherweise keine Verlaufsform:
hear   see
(Aber: *to listen* (= **zu**hören) und *to watch* (= **zu**sehen) sind **Tätigkeitsverben** und haben deshalb auch eine **Verlaufsform**.)

29. Fülle die Lücken!

Denk daran, dass *think* beides sein kann: ein **Tätigkeitsverb** (T) und ein **Zustandsverb** (Z). Wenn du es mit der Verlaufsform verwendest, ist es ein Tätigkeitsverb und bedeutet *nachdenken*. Wenn du es mit der einfachen Form verwendest, ist es ein Zustandsverb und bedeutet *davon halten*.

Beispiele:

What **are** you **thinking** about? → Worüber denkst du gerade nach? (T)
What **do** you **think** of it?   → Was hältst du davon? (Z)

1. "What ....you ....of this new CD?" – "It's great!"
2. "What ....you ....about?" – "I ....about the test tomorrow."
3. "What ....you ....of the new teacher?" – "He is boring!"
4. "What ....you ....about?" – "I ....about my mum. She's in hospital."

I'm having a bath.

30. Wo heißt es *have* und wo *am having*?

Denk daran, dass **to have** nur dann keine Verlaufsform hat, wenn es *besitzen* heißt. Manchmal taucht es aber auch in Ausdrücken auf und bedeutet dann **nicht** *besitzen*, z. B.: *to have a bath*. Dann kann es natürlich eine Verlaufsform haben, denn es kann ja sein, dass jemand gerade dabei ist zu baden!

1. "Are you enjoying the party?" – "Yes, I _____ a lot of fun."
2. "I _____ a new car. It is a Japanese car."
3. "Where are you?" – "I'm in the bathroom. I _____ a shower."
4. "Are you ready to go?" – "No, I _____ breakfast."

31. Wie kannst du diese Sätze und Fragen ins Englische übersetzen?
1. Jetzt verstehe ich. _____
2. Jetzt erinnere ich mich. _____
3. Jetzt weiß ich. _____
4. Worüber denkt sie gerade nach? _____

present simple oder present progressive

Die einfache Form:

Das *present simple* drückt aus, dass etwas **regelmäßig** passiert oder dass jemand etwas **gewohnheitsmäßig** oder **nie** tut.

• zusätzliche Erkennungszeichen: Wörter wie *always, usually, often, sometimes, never, every day, every year*

Die Verlaufsform:

Das *present progressive* drückt aus, dass **gerade** etwas passiert oder dass jemand gerade dabei ist, etwas zu tun.

• zusätzliche Erkennungszeichen: Wörter wie *at the moment, now* manchmal auch: *today, this morning, this week*

Es fällt dir sicher bald ganz leicht zu entscheiden, welche Form der Gegenwart du brauchst, wenn du mit Hilfe der Zeichnung auf alle Punkte achtest.

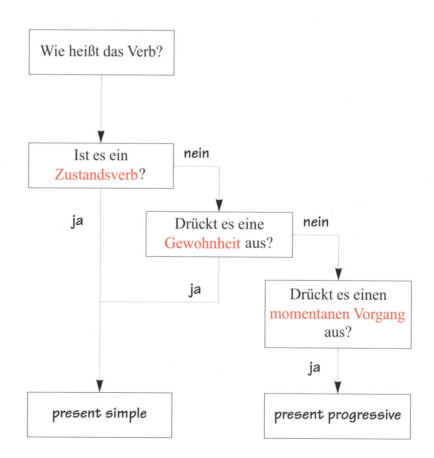

32. Lisa und Tom stellen zwei ähnliche Fragen, die sich aber in der Zeitform unterscheiden. Daran kannst du erkennen, wie du sie diesen deutschen Sätzen zuordnen musst:

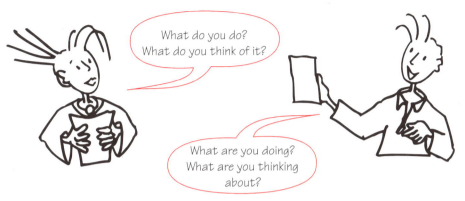

1. Wie denkst du darüber? Was hältst du davon?

   _____

2. Worüber denkst du nach?

   _____

3. Was machst du (beruflich)?

   _____

4. Was machst du (gerade)?

   _____

33. Vervollständige die Sätze mit der richtigen Form des Präsens!
1. (to come) "Hurry up! We're late." – "OK, I _____ ."
2. (to speak, not / to understand) Caroline usually _____ so quickly that I _____ her.
3. (to drink, to drink) She usually _____ tea but today she _____ coffee.
4. (to have) Alison _____ a bath every Saturday.
5. (to have) "Where is Alison?" – "She's in the bathroom. She _____ a bath."
6. (to love) "_____ you _____ her?"
7. (to go) Raymond always _____ to bed at ten o'clock.
8. (to go) "Good night! I _____ to bed now."
9. (to learn) Most people _____ to ride a bicycle when they are children.
10. (to learn) Carmen is in England at the moment. She _____ English.
11. (not / to rain) It _____ very much in the Sahara.
12. (not / to rain) "Let's go for a walk. It _____ now."

Vergangenheit

to be: was / were

They were on the beach last weekend.

einfache Vergangenheit von to be – bejahte Form

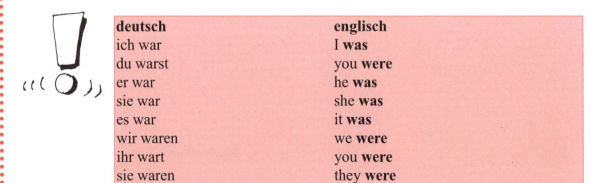

deutsch	englisch
ich war	I **was**
du warst	you **were**
er war	he **was**
sie war	she **was**
es war	it **was**
wir waren	we **were**
ihr wart	you **were**
sie waren	they **were**

34. Setze in die Lücke *was* oder *were* ein:

1. He _____ very angry yesterday.
2. It _____ all right.
3. We _____ on holiday last week.
4. I _____ in Canada two years ago.
5. They _____ very tired yesterday.

35. Versuche nun, die folgenden Sätze ins Englische zu übersetzen.

1. Diese Schuhe waren teuer.

_____

2. Letztes Jahr waren wir in York.

_____

3. Letzte Woche war ich in Birmingham.

_____

4. Sie war glücklich.

_____

5. Es war langweilig.

_____

36. Wie kannst du auf Englisch sagen, wo die Leute gestern waren?
Verwende diese Wörter dabei: in hospital   in bed   ill   at school
at the hotel   at the museum

1. Ihr wart in der Schule.

_____

2. Ich war krank. Ich war im Bett.

_____

3. Wir waren im Krankenhaus.

_____

4. Er war im Hotel.

_____

5. Sie waren im Museum.

_____

He wasn't at the party.

einfache Vergangenheit von to be – verneinte Form

deutsch	Langform	Kurzform
ich war nicht	I **was not**	I **wasn't**
du warst nicht	you **were not**	you **weren't**
er war nicht	he **was not**	he **wasn't**
sie war nicht	she **was not**	she **wasn't**
es war nicht	it **was not**	it **wasn't**
wir waren nicht	we **were not**	we **weren't**
ihr wart nicht	you **were not**	you **weren't**
sie waren nicht	they **were not**	they **weren't**

37. Was gehört in die Lücke: *wasn't* oder *weren't*?

1. He _____wasn't_____ funny.
2. She _____wasn't_____ frightened.
3. They _____weren't_____ early.
4. I _____wasn't_____ late.
5. It _____wasn't_____ boring.

38. Erzähle mit Hilfe der untenstehenden Wörter auf Englisch, wo Tom und Lisa gestern waren bzw. nicht waren.

at the restaurant   at work   at a party   at the cinema   at home

1. Tom und Lisa waren nicht im Kino.
   Tom and Lisa weren't at the cinema.
2. Lisa war nicht bei der Arbeit.
   Lisa wasn't at work.
3. Tom war nicht zu Hause.
   Tom wasn't at home.
4. Tom und Lisa waren nicht im Restaurant.
   Tom and Lisa weren't at the restaurant.
5. Sie waren auf einer Party!
   You weren't at the party.

39. Die Millars waren im Urlaub und sind nicht zufrieden. Sage die folgenden Sätze auf Englisch!
Diese Wörter solltest du benutzen: not warm enough   not nice enough not big enough   not clean enough   not cheap enough

1. Das Essen war nicht billig genug.
   The food weren't cheap enough.
2. Das Wasser im See war nicht warm genug.
   The See wasn't warm enough.
3. Die Zimmer waren nicht sauber genug.
   The room wasn't clean enough.
4. Das Schwimmbad war nicht groß genug.
   The swimmingpool wasn't big enough.
5. Das Wetter war nicht gut genug.
   The weather wasn't nice enough.

Was your exam difficult?

einfache Vergangenheit von to be – Frageform und Kurzantwort:

deutsche Frage	englische Frage	Kurzantwort
war ich ?	**was** I ?	Yes, I was. / No, I wasn't.
warst du ?	**were** you ?	Yes, you were. / No, you weren't.
war er ?	**was** he ?	Yes, he was. / No, he wasn't.
war sie ?	**was** she ?	Yes, she was. / No, she wasn't.
war es ?	**was** it ?	Yes, it was. / No, it wasn't.
waren wir ?	**were** we ?	Yes, we were. / No, we weren't.
wart ihr ?	**were** you ?	Yes, you were. / No, you weren't.
waren sie ?	**were** they ?	Yes, they were. / No, they weren't.

40. Welche Form von *to be* musst du in die erste Lücke und welche in die zweite eintragen?

1. _____ it nice?   Yes, it _____ .
2. _____ the people friendly?   Yes, they _____ .
3. _____ there any dogs?   Yes, there _____ .
4. _____ you afraid?   No, I _____ .
5. _____ you homesick?   No, I _____ .

41. Stelle auf Englisch Fragen zu dem, was da gesagt wird.
Beispiel: I saw a monster last night. (frightened?)
             → Were you frightened?

1. I read two books about Winnie-the-Pooh. (interesting?)

_____

2. I went to the South Pole last year. (cold?)

_____

3. I didn't sleep much last week. (tired?)

_____

4. I went to the sauna last Monday. (hot?)

_____

5. I had two tests yesterday. (difficult?)

_____

42. Bilde nun Fragen mit Fragewörtern!
Diese Fragewörter können gebraucht werden: *when what where who why*

1. Wo wart ihr?

_____

2. Was war das Problem?

_____

3. Warum warst du so ärgerlich?

_____

4. Wann war das?

_____

5. Wer war gestern im Kino?

_____

past simple

Diese Vergangenheitsform verwendest du, wenn du
- über **vergangene Ereignisse oder Erlebnisse** berichtest,
- eine Geschichte erzählst

oder wenn du sagst,
- **wann** jemand etwas gemacht hat oder
- **wann** etwas geschehen ist.

He looked at the picture.

Die meisten Verben sind **regelmäßig**. Das bedeutet, dass du einfach *-ed* an die englische Grundform anhängst und fertig!

deutsche Grundform	englische Grundform	simple past
arbeiten	(to) work	worked
regnen	(to) rain	rained

Im Deutschen müssen dann immer noch verschiedene Endungen angehängt werden. Und im Englischen nicht. Auf Englisch ist es also viel einfacher! Beispiel:

ich kam an	du kam**st** an	er/sie/es kam an
*I arriv**ed***	*you arriv**ed***	*he/she/it arriv**ed***
wir kam**en** an	ihr kam**t** an	sie kam**en** an
*we arriv**ed***	*you arriv**ed***	*they arriv**ed***

Manchmal musst du aber gut aufpassen, dass du die **ed-Form** richtig schreibst:
- **stummes *-e* am Ende fällt weg:** *to phone* + -ed → *phoned*
- ***-el* am Ende wird verdoppelt:** *to travel* + -ed → *travelled*
- **Konsonant + *-y* am Ende wird zu Konsonant + *-ied*:**
  to try + -ed → *tried*
- **Vokal + *-y* am Ende wird zu Vokal + *-yed*:**
  to play + -ed → *played*
- **Ein einfacher Konsonant** am Ende wird nach **kurzem, einfachem und betontem Vokal verdoppelt:** *to stop* + -ed → *stopped*

43. Bilde die einfache Vergangenheitsform und fülle die Lücken mit den richtigen Wörtern:

to bark to happen to want to live to start to move to stay
to wait to start to park to try to save to finish to watch
to enjoy to walk

1. I wasn't well yesterday so I _____ stayed _____ in bed.
2. The film _____ started _____ at 8 o'clock and it _____ finished _____ at 10 o'clock.
3. The dog _____ barked _____ at the cat.
4. Princess Diana _____ lived _____ from 1961 to 1997.
5. The accident _____ happened _____ last night.
6. The Robsons don't live here anymore. They _____ ~~saved~~ moved _____ to Dublin last summer.
7. They _____ wanted _____ to go for a walk but then it _____ started _____ to rain.
8. She _____ parked _____ the car outside the restaurant.
9. Last night we _____ watched _____ television. The film wasn't very good.
10. The ambulance men _____ started _____ the man's life.
11. Vivienne was late but her friends _____ waited _____ for her.
12. We _____ enjoyed _____ our holiday in Ireland. The people were very friendly.
13. There was no bus so they _____ moved _____ home.
14. He _____ tryed _____ to answer the question but it was too difficult.

44. Diese Woche war **alles anders als sonst**. Fülle die Lücken mit der **einfachen Vergangenheitsform** dieser Wörter:

to shout to walk to rain to play to help

1. We usually play hockey but this Saturday we _____ played _____ golf.
2. We usually take the bus to school but this week we _____ ~~hab~~ walked _____ to school.
3. We usually help in the kitchen but yesterday we _____ helped _____ in the garden.
4. It usually doesn't rain much in the summer but this week it _____ rained _____ every day.
5. My teacher doesn't usually shout at me but yesterday he _____ shouted _____ at me.

Unregelmäßige Verben

Es gibt auch einige englische Verben, die ihre Vergangenheitsformen nicht regelmäßig bilden. Im Deutschen ist das ja genauso. Da heißt es zwar:

ich lache – ich lach**te** – ich **habe ge**lach**t**, und

ich sage – ich sag**te** – ich **habe ge**sag**t**.

aber: ich bin – ich war – ich bin gewesen

(und **nicht** ich bin – ich bin**te** – ich **habe** gebint!)

Das Ganze ist gar nicht so schwer. Es gibt nämlich Listen, in denen steht, wie die Formen heißen müssen. In deinem Schulbuch ist sicher eine drin, die so ähnlich aussieht:

| deutsch | englisch | | |
Infinitiv	*Infinitiv*	*simple past*	*past participle*
sein	*be (am/is/are)*	*was*	*been*
kaufen	*buy*	*bought*	*bought*
tun	*do*	*did*	*done*
bekommen, werden	*get*	*got*	*got*
gehen	*go*	*went*	*gone*
lesen	*read*	*read*	*read*
singen	*sing*	*sang*	*sung*
unterichten, lehren	*teach*	*taught*	*taught*

Wie du siehst, stehen da für jedes deutsche Wort **drei Formen**. Die erste davon ist der **Infinitiv**, also die Grundform. Diese Form kennst du ja bereits. Wenn du nun einen Satz in der einfachen Vergangenheit bilden möchtest, dann brauchst du dafür immer die zweite Form, das sogenannte *simple past*. Die kannst du in so einer Liste sicher leicht finden.

Beispiel: die zweite Form von **to go** (= gehen) heißt auf Englisch **went**.

Wenn du es gefunden hast, dann kannst du das Wort wieder einfach in den Satz stecken! Ganz ohne Endungen!

Damit du gut üben kannst und dich auch gut abhören lassen kannst, ist hinten in diesem Buch eine **Liste mit den wichtigsten unregelmäßigen Verben** abgedruckt. Je mehr du davon auswendig weißt, desto besser!

45. Ordne diese Wörter richtig zu!

~~forgot~~ ~~knew~~ ~~thought~~ ~~told~~ ~~wrote~~ ~~drank~~ ~~made~~ ~~won~~ ~~spent~~ ~~went~~

Fülle die Lücken mit der richtigen Verbform:

1. I have a headache because I ___drank___ some red wine last night.
2. They ___went___ to Kathleen's party last Saturday.
3. The teacher asked a lot of questions. Peter ___knew___ all the answers.
4. Phil ___made___ a cake for Linda's birthday.
5. We went shopping. We ___spent___ a lot of money.
6. Is it your birthday today? I ___thought___ it was on Friday!
7. He ___told___ his parents about his new job.
8. Mrs. Millar is angry because I ___forgot___ to do my homework.
9. Michael took part in a race last Saturday. He ___won___ the race.
10. My pen-friend ___wrote___ me a very nice letter.

46. Was machte Lisa in der letzten Zeit? Fülle die Lücken mit der einfachen Vergangenheitsform:

Beispiel: to go Lisa: *I **went** to New York last year.*

1. to find
   I ___found___ an earring yesterday.
2. to run
   I ___ran___ all the way to school this morning.
3. to fall
   I ___falled___ off my bicycle this afternoon.
4. to hurt
   and I ___hured___ my arm.
5. to hear
   I ___hered___ the bell not long ago.
6. to pay
   I ___payed___ for my ice-cream.
7. to fly
   I ___floied___ to Manchester last month.
8. to buy
   I ___bought___ a nice coat yesterday.
9. to wear
   I ___weared___ my new dress on Saturday evening.
10. to understand
    I ___understood___ the instructions the teacher gave us.

I didn't go to the doctor.

Für solche **verneinten** Sätze im **past simple** brauchst du fast das Gleiche wie beim **present simple**. Der einzige Unterschied ist, dass es statt *do* oder *does* nun immer *did* heißen muss.

Für solche verneinten Sätze im **past simple** brauchst du die richtige Form

von   to do +   not +   Infinitiv

Gegenwart: He   do**es**   not   play   chess.   (Er spielt nicht Schach.)
past: He   **did**   not   play   chess.   (Er spielte nicht Schach.)

He didn't have dinner. He didn't eat the vegetables. He didn't like the steak. He didn't want anything to drink.

past simple – verneinte Form:

deutsch	englische Langform	englische Kurzform
ich spielte nicht	I **did not play**	I **didn't play**
du spieltest nicht	you **did not play**	you **didn't play**
er spielte nicht	he **did not play**	he **didn't play**
sie spielte nicht	she **did not play**	she **didn't play**
es spielte nicht	it **did not play**	it **didn't play**
wir spielten nicht	we **did not play**	we **didn't play**
ihr spieltet nicht	you **did not play**	you **didn't play**
sie spielten nicht	they **did not play**	they **didn't play**

Wie du siehst, ist es einfacher als im Deutschen. Im Englischen wird in dieser Zeit bei *he*, *she* oder *it* und bei allen anderen Formen **NICHTS** angehängt!

47. Verneine diese Sätze:

She saw a monster last night. *She didn't see a monster last night.*

1. The red car overtook the blue one.

2. He fed the animals. He didn't ~~feed~~ the animals.

3. You ate meat. You didn't ~~ate~~ eat meat.

4. They bought a magazine.

5. She swam to the other side of the lake.

6. He wrote me a letter yesterday.

7. They forgot to buy a present.

8. She sold her bicycle to a friend.

9. They spent a lot of money.

10. Mrs. Williams taught Spanish.

11. He drew a nice picture.

12. We went to a restaurant.

48. Und was hast du gestern gemacht? Schreibe einen **bejahten** Satz, wenn du etwas gestern gemacht hast, und wenn nicht, dann schreibst du einen **verneinten** Satz, z. B.: *to have breakfast*

I had breakfast. oder: *I didn't have breakfast.*

1. to get up before 8 o'clock — I didn't
2. to go to school — had go to school.
3. to speak English — had speak English
4. to do your homework — I had my homework.
5. to bake a cake
6. to do the shopping
7. to play football
8. to listen to music
9. to have a bath
10. to go to the cinema

43

Did you have a good holiday?

past simple – Frageform und Kurzantwort:

deutsch	englisch	Kurzantwort
Hatte ich ... ?	**Did** I **have** ... ?	Yes, I **did**. / No, I **didn't**.
Hattest du ... ?	**Did** you **have**... ?	Yes, you **did**. / No, you **didn't**.
Hatte er ... ?	**Did** he **have**... ?	Yes, he **did**. / No, he **didn't**.
Hatte sie ... ?	**Did** she **have**... ?	Yes, she **did**. / No, she **didn't**.
Hatte es ... ?	**Did** it **have**... ?	Yes, it **did**. / No, it **didn't**.
Hatten wir .. ?	**Did** we **have**... ?	Yes, we **did**. / No, we **didn't**.
Hattet ihr ... ?	**Did** you **have**... ?	Yes, you **did**. / No, you **didn't**.
Hatten sie ... ?	**Did** they **have**... ?	Yes, they **did**. / No, they **didn't**.

49. Was hast du gestern gemacht? Schreibe **wahre** Kurzantworten!
Beispiel: Did you have breakfast? *Yes, I did.* oder *No, I didn't.*

1. Did you get up early? No _____
2. Did you have a shower? _____
3. Did you meet some of your friends? _____
4. Did you watch a video? _____
5. Did you go ice-skating? _____

50. Du möchtest wissen, ob andere das Gleiche erlebt haben wie du. Bilde die richtigen Fragen:
Beispiel: I slept very well last week. And you? *Did you sleep very well?*

1. I heard a strange noise last night. And you? _____?
2. I saw a ghost. And you? _____?
3. I ran away. And you? _____?
4. I hid under the bed. And you? _____?
5. I stayed there all night. And you? _____?

51. Bilde Fragen mit **Fragewörtern**.
Beispiel: I found something. *What did you find?*

1. I bought a magazine
Which magazine ___did___ you ___buy___ ?
2. They left the room.
Why _____?
3. I phoned you.
When _____ you _____?
4. It didn't take very long.
How long _____?
5. I spent a lot of money.
How much _____ you _____?
6. He arrived early.
What time _____?
7. I met somebody.
Who _____ you _____?
8. She chose a new bicyle.
Which one _____?
9. I went out.
Where _____ you _____?
10. They had breakfast.
What _____ for breakfast?

past progressive

Wenn du ausdrücken möchtest, dass eine Aktivität in der Vergangenheit andauerte oder dass sie bereits im Gange war, dann brauchst du im Deutschen meistens zusätzliche Wörter.

Du kannst dann zum Beispiel sagen:

> *Er war am Telefonieren.*

oder: *Er war gerade dabei zu telefonieren, als …*

Wenn du auf Englisch ausdrücken möchtest, dass

- etwas in der Vergangenheit stattfand und eine Zeit lang andauerte, oder
- etwas zu einem Zeitpunkt in der Vergangenheit bereits im Gange war, oder
- etwas bereits im Gange war, als eine andere Aktivität einsetzte oder etwas geschah,

dann brauchst du keine zusätzlichen Wörter, sondern nur eine bestimmte Verbform: das sogenannte **past progressive** in der bejahten Form. Manchmal sagen deine Lehrerinnen oder Lehrer vielleicht auch **past continuous** dazu, damit ist aber das Gleiche gemeint.

I was watching a film at 7 o'clock.

Die Form ist gar nicht schwierig – sie ist ganz ähnlich wie das *present progressive*. Du brauchst jetzt bloß entweder **was** oder **were** – und dann die **ing-Form**, die du ja schon aus dem speziellen ing-Form-Kapitel gut kennst.

past progressive – bejahte Form:

deutsch	englisch
ich war (gerade) dabei zu essen	I **was** eat**ing**
du warst (gerade) dabei zu essen	you **were** eat**ing**
er war (gerade) dabei zu essen	he **was** eat**ing**
sie war (gerade) dabei zu essen	she **was** eat**ing**
es war (gerade) dabei zu essen	it **was** eat**ing**
wir waren (gerade) dabei zu essen	we **were** eat**ing**
ihr wart (gerade) dabei zu essen	you **were** eat**ing**
sie waren (gerade) dabei zu essen	they **were** eat**ing**

52. In das Haus von Lisa und Tom ist gestern abend um sieben Uhr eingebrochen worden. Am nächsten Morgen fragt ein Polizist alle in der Straße, was sie um diese Zeit gemacht haben. Alle sagen, dass sie ein Alibi haben.
WER WAR'S?

What were you doing yesterday evening at seven o'clock?

Vervollständige die Sätze:

1. (to do) Policeman: "Good morning. I am afraid I must ask everybody what they _____ yesterday evening at seven o'clock."
2. (to play) Mr. and Mrs. Carlisle: "We _____ cards with the Deans."
3. (to feed) Jean: "I _____ my hamster."
4. (to read) Barbara: "I _____ chapter 2 of Winnie-the-Pooh."
5. (to have) Christopher and Robin: "We _____ a bath."
6. (to take) William: "I _____ the dog for a walk."
7. (to do) Shelley: "I _____ my homework."
8. (to prepare) Mr. and Mrs. McIntyre: "We _____ dinner."
9. (to work) Richard: "I _____ on my computer."
10. (to watch) Mr. Carmichael: "I _____ TV with the Carlisles."
11. (to wash) Miss Moore: "I _____ my hair".
12. (to write) Claudia: "I _____ to my pen-friend."
13. (to look for) Joy: "I _____ my cat."
14. (to teach) Mrs. White: "I _____ an evening class."
15. (to talk) Debbie: "I _____ to my friend Charlene."
16. (to drive) Mr. and Mrs. Johnston: "We _____ home from work."
17. (to play) Mr. and Mrs. Dean: "We _____ cards with the Carlisles."
18. (to repair) Jan and Eric: "We _____ our bicycles."
19. (to listen) Kevin: "I _____ to my new CD."
20. (to take part in) Phil: "I _____ a table-tennis match."

She wasn't listening.

Wenn du auf Englisch ausdrücken möchtest, dass
- ein Vorgang in der Vergangenheit nicht stattfand und
- nicht eine Zeit lang andauerte, oder dass
- etwas zu einem Zeitpunkt in der Vergangenheit nicht bereits im Gange war, oder dass
- etwas nicht bereits im Gange war, als eine andere Aktivität einsetzte,

dann brauchst du auch das sogenannte **past progressive** – aber in der **verneinten Form**.

I'm sorry. I wasn't looking.

past progressive – verneinte Form:

englische Langform	englische Kurzform
I **was not** work**ing**	I **wasn't** work**ing**
you **were not** work**ing**	you **weren't** work**ing**
he **was not** work**ing**	he **wasn't** work**ing**
she **was not** work**ing**	she **wasn't** work**ing**
it **was not** work**ing**	it **wasn't** work**ing**
we **were not** work**ing**	we **weren't** work**ing**
you **were not** work**ing**	you **weren't** work**ing**
they **were not** work**ing**	they **weren't** work**ing**

53. Verneine diese Sätze:
1. Maggie was practising the clarinet.

   _____

2. Andrew was baking a cake.

   _____

3. Isobel and Richard were driving home.

   _____

4. Darren was playing football.

   _____

5. Shireen was teaching French.

   _____

54. Chaos in der Klasse! Der Schulleiter kam gestern zum Geografieunter-
richt, aber niemand machte gerade das, was er oder sie machen sollte!
Vervollständige diese Sätze!
1. (not / to clean) Elaine _____ the board.
2. (not / to read) Colin and Alan _____ the text.
3. (not / to do) Perry and Ross _____ their
   project work.
4. (not / to listen) David _____ to his teacher.
5. (not / to use) Lindsay and Joanne _____ their
   maps.

55. Vervollständige die folgenden Sätze!
Beispiele:
James: (–) to play the clarinet … James wasn't playing the clarinet, …
        (+) to play the piano … he was playing the piano. …
1. Sharon: (–) to ride a bicycle,

   _____

   (+) to ride a horse.

   _____

2. Nigel: (–) to play hockey,

   _____

   (+) to play rugby.

   _____

3. Judy: (–) to read Shakespeare,

   _____

   (+) to read comics.

   _____

Were you working?

Bei **Entscheidungsfragen** werden einfach nur wieder - wie zum Beispiel im *present progressive* – die Plätze getauscht:

Aussagesatz: He   was   watching TV.

Fragesatz: Was   he   watching TV?

past progressive – Frageform und Kurzantwort:

englische Frage	Kurzantwort
was I watch**ing**?	**Yes, I was. / No, I wasn't.**
were you watch**ing**?	**Yes, you were. / No, you weren't.**
was he watch**ing**?	**Yes, he was. / No, he wasn't.**
was she watch**ing**?	**Yes, she was. / No, she wasn't.**
was it watch**ing**?	**Yes, it was. / No, it wasn't.**
were we watch**ing**?	**Yes, we were. / No, we weren't.**
were you watch**ing**?	**Yes, you were. / No, you weren't.**
were they watch**ing**?	**Yes, they were. / No, they weren't.**

Fragen mit Fragewörtern:

What … ? (*Was? / Welche?*)   What **was** John **doing**?
                                 What **were** they **buying**?

Where … ? (*Wo?*)   Where **were** they **staying**?
                                 Where **was** she **going**?

Why … ? (*Warum?*)   Why **were** you **crying**?
                                 Why **was** he **getting** up?

56. Vervollständige die Fragen:

1. (to play) _____ they _____ volleyball?
2. (to work) _____ she _____ all day yesterday?
3. (to shine) _____ the sun _____ when you went out?
4. (to sleep) _____ he still _____ when you arrived?
5. (to have) _____ you _____ lunch when the phone rang?

57. Was hast du vorgestern um 14 Uhr gemacht? Schreibe wahre Kurzantworten!

1. Were you having lunch?
   _____

2. Were you doing your homework?
   _____

3. Were you reading a book?
   _____

4. Were you playing tennis?
   _____

5. Were you playing football?
   _____

58. Du möchtest wissen, was verschiedene Leute gerade gemacht haben, als gestern plötzlich der Strom ausfiel? Wie kannst du diese Fragen auf Englisch stellen?

1. „Warst du gerade dabei fernzusehen?"
   _____

2. „Warst du gerade dabei, ein Buch zu lesen?"
   _____

3. „Warst du gerade dabei, dein Fahrrad zu reparieren?"
   _____

4. „Warst du gerade dabei, einen Kuchen zu backen?"
   _____

5. „Warst du gerade dabei zu baden?"
   _____

past simple oder past progressive

Die einfache Form der Vergangenheit drückt aus:
- **wann** jemand etwas getan hat oder wann etwas geschehen ist und dass die Ereignisse oder Handlungen **abgeschlossen** oder **vorbei** sind
- dass mehreres in der Vergangenheit **nacheinander** erfolgte
- zusätzliche Erkennungszeichen. Wörter wie: *yesterday*, *last week*, *five minutes ago*.

Die Verlaufsform der Vergangenheit drückt aus:
- die **Entwicklung** und den Verlauf von etwas und das „wann" ist nicht so wichtig, sondern, dass es **eine Zeit lang andauerte**, oder dass mehreres **gleichzeitig** ausgeführt wurde
- **Hintergrundhandlungen** oder Begleitumstände

Stehen **beide Zeitformen in einem Satz**, so steht für das Hintergrundgeschehen (das womit man gerade beschäftigt war) → *progressive* und für die plötzliche oder überraschende Aktion (... als ..., ... als plötzlich ...) → *simple*.

Dieser Fragebaum hilft dir bei der Entscheidung.

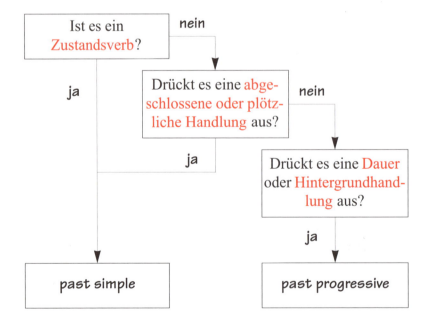

59. Fülle die Lücken mit den angegebenen Verben aus. Wie geschahen diese Aktionen?

Alles nacheinander? → *past simple*
Alles gleichzeitig? → *past progressive*

1. This morning they ____got____ up, then they ____washed____, ____put____ on their clothes and ____had____ breakfast (to get, to wash, to put, to have). Then they ____went____ to school (to go). There they ____worked____ on their history project (to work). Then they ____had____ maths and then they ____had____ a French test (to have, to have). Then they ____went____ home again (to go).

2. At 5 o'clock, Janice ____was listening____ to her new CDs and Vanessa ____was playing____ tennis (to listen, to play). Stewart ____was playing____ football and Tom ____was playing____ a computer game (to play, to play). Mum ____was washing____ the car and Dad ____was preparing____ their dinner (to wash, to prepare). Grandmother ____was reading____ a newspaper (to read).

I *was playing* a computer game **when** Lisa *came* in.

Hintergrundgeschehen,
Tätigkeit im Verlauf
(→ *past progressive*)

2. Handlung,
eine Art *Unterbrechung*
als … (→ *past simple*)

60. Was gehört in welche Lücke? War eine Handlung schon im Gange, als die zweite einsetzte?

1. I ____was having____ a bath **when** the phone ____rang____ (to have, to ring).

2. **When** they ____went____ out, the sun ____was shining____ (to go, to shine).

3. They ____were sitting____ in the garden **when** it ____started____ to rain (to sit, to start).

4. Jack ____was walking____ down the street **when** he suddenly ____saw____ an elephant (to walk, to see).

5. While I ____was driving____ to work this morning I almost ____had____ a very bad accident (to drive, to have).

present perfect simple

Diese Vergangenheitsform verwendest du, wenn du
- von etwas berichtest, was zwar **in der Vergangenheit angefangen** hat, aber noch irgendwie **in die Gegenwart hineinreicht,**
- **über vergangene Ereignisse oder Erlebnisse berichtest,** es dich aber nicht interessiert, wann genau es passiert ist,
- du vor allem Interesse daran hast, welche **Auswirkung es auf die Gegenwart** hat.
- zusätzliche Erkennungszeichen sind Wörter wie z. B.: *already* (schon), *ever* (jemals), *just* (gerade), *never* (bisher noch nie), *not yet* (bis jetzt noch nicht), *yet* (bis jetzt). Sie alle zeigen dir an, dass sich die Handlung irgendwie auf die Gegenwart auswirkt.

He has broken his leg.

Das **deutsche Perfekt** wird manchmal mit **sein** gebildet, z. B.: *er ist gefallen, wir sind gewesen*; manchmal mit *haben*, z. B.: *sie hat gelacht, ihr habt getanzt*. Das **englische present perfect** wird **immer mit** *to have* gebildet – da ist es also viel, viel einfacher!

present perfect simple – bejahte Form:

Langform	Kurzform
I **have** finish**ed**	I**'ve** finish**ed**
you **have** finish**ed**	you**'ve** finish**ed**
he **has** finish**ed**	he**'s** finish**ed**
she **has** finish**ed**	she**'s** finish**ed**
it **has** finish**ed**	it**'s** finish**ed**
we **have** finish**ed**	we**'ve** finish**ed**
you **have** finish**ed**	you**'ve** finish**ed**
they **have** finish**ed**	they**'ve** finish**ed**

Wie du siehst brauchst du für diese Form **has** (oder **have**) und dann das sogenannte **Partizip Perfekt**. Das ist bei den regelmäßigen Verben die *ed*-Form und bei den unregelmäßigen Verben die Form in der dritten englischen Spalte. Die findest du in der Liste der unregelmäßigen Verben in deinem Schulbuch oder hinten in diesem Buch.

61. Bringe die Satzteile in die richtige Reihenfolge, so dass sinnvolle Sätze entstehen:

1. busy / been / have / very / We / .

   We have been very busy

2. to / has / written / He / me / .

   He has written to me

3. We / wonderful / had / holiday / have / a / .

   We have had a wonderful holiday

4. five / drunk / of / I / cups / have / tea / already / .

   I have drunk five cups of tea, already

5. gone / has / just / out / He / .

   He has just gone out.

6. him / phoned / She / has / already / .

   She has already phoned him.

7. made / have / just / coffee / I / some / .

   I have just made some coffee

8. times / you / already / We / three / asked / have / .

   We have already asked you three times

9. her / just / bicycle / repaired / She / has / .

   She has just repaird her bicycle

10. Japan / been / never / have / to / They / .

    They have never been to Japan

62. Joanne hatte einen Unfall und liegt im Krankenhaus. Sie macht sich Sorgen, wie es bei ihr zu Hause aussieht und wie es ihren Haustieren geht. Anne besucht sie und erzählt ihr, dass alles in Ordnung ist, weil jeder von ihren Freunden *gerade eine Aufgabe erledigt hat.* Vervollständige die Sätze:

1. (to do) Cathleen _____ the washing.
2. (to wash) Carl _____ the dishes.
3. (to dry) Maeve _____ _dried_ _____ the dishes.
4. (to wash) Ann and Susan _____ all the floors.
5. (to phone) Bill _____ the milkman.
6. (to water) Ken _____ the vegetables in the garden.
7. (to buy) Jocelyn _____ _baught_ _____ some cat food and some dog food.
8. (to feed) Richard _____ _fed_ _____ the cat and the dog.
9. (to take) Bruce and Gavin _____ the dog for a walk.
10. (to bring) Robin and I _____ _braught_ _____ you all your postcards and letters.

I haven't been to the disco for three weeks.

We haven't had a holiday for two years.

We haven't had a holiday for millions of light years.

present perfect simple – verneinte Form:

Langform	Kurzform
I **have not** started	I **haven't** started
you **have not** started	you **haven't** started
he **has not** started	he **hasn't** started
she **has not** started	she **hasn't** started
it **has not** started	it **hasn't** started
we **have not** started	we **haven't** started
you **have not** started	you **haven't** started
they **have not** started	they **haven't** started

Zeitangaben:

Im Perfekt werden oft Aussagen darüber gemacht, **wie lange schon** oder **seit wann** etwas geschieht … oder nicht geschieht!

I haven't seen him **for** six months. (→ wie lange schon, **Zeitdauer**)

since December 29th. (→ seit wann, **Zeitpunkt**)

Pass gut auf:

- *for* mit Zeitdauer! (for an hour, for 30 minutes, for two days, for 65 years, etc.)
- *since* mit Zeitpunkt! (since 7 o'clock, since Wednesday, since lunchtime, etc.)

63. Verneine diese Sätze!

1. I have tried to learn English.
   I haven't tried to learn English
2. Helen has gone home.
   Helen hasn't gone home
3. We have found the answer.
   We haven't found the answer
4. I have finished this exercise.
   I haven't finished this exercise
5. Alan has been to the cinema.
   Alan hasn't been to the cinema.

64. **for** oder **since**? Fülle die Lücken.

1. I haven't written any letters _____for_____ many years.
2. He hasn't spoken a word _____since_____ 6 o'clock.
3. I haven't spoken French _____since_____ 1996.
4. We haven't eaten in a restaurant _____for_____ a long time.
5. Dad hasn't ridden a bicycle _____since for_____ 30 years.
6. They haven't eaten any chocolate eggs _____for since_____ Easter.
7. She hasn't answered the phone _____for_____ hours.
8. I haven't heard from him _____since_____ Sunday.
9. They haven't milked the cows _____since_____ breakfast-time.
10. The phone hasn't rung _____for_____ 20 minutes.

65. Wie kannst du diese Sätze auf Englisch sagen?

1. Geoffrey hat seine Schlüssel noch nicht gefunden.
   Geoffrey hasn't been find his key
2. Sie haben das Haus jahrelang nicht sauber gemacht.
   They haven't been washing there house for a long time.
3. Perry hat das Buch noch nicht gelesen.
   Perry hasn't been read the book
4. Jason hat Kylie seit zwei Wochen nicht gesehen.
   Jason hasn't been seeing Kylie for two weeks
5. Francis hat die Katze noch nicht gefüttert.
   Francis hasn't been feeding the cat.

Has it stopped raining yet?

Bei **Entscheidungsfragen** werden einfach nur wieder die Plätze getauscht:

Aussagesatz: She has gone out.

Fragesatz: **Has she** gone out?

Have you ever seen the Loch Ness monster?

Yes, I have.

present perfect simple – Frageform und Kurzantwort:

englische Frage	Kurzantwort
have I finish**ed**?	Yes, I **have**. / No, I **haven't**.
have you finish**ed**?	Yes, you **have**. / No, you **haven't**.
has he finish**ed**?	Yes, he **has**. / No, he **hasn't**.
has she finish**ed**?	Yes, she **has**. / No, she **hasn't**.
has it finish**ed**?	Yes, it **has**. / No, it **hasn't**.
have we finish**ed**?	Yes, we **have**. / No, we **haven't**.
have you finish**ed**?	Yes, you **have**. / No, you **haven't**.
have they finish**ed**?	Yes, they **have**. / No, they **haven't**.

Beispiele für Fragen mit Fragewörtern:

What … ? (*Was? / Welche?*)   What have you done?

Where … (*Wo?*)   Where have you been?

How many … ? (*Wie viele?*)   How many letters have you written?

66. Schreibe wahre Kurzantworten:

1. Have you ever lost any money?

   _____

2. Have you ever slept in a tent?

   _____

3. Have you ever been to Scotland?

   _____

4. Have you ever eaten Chinese food?

   _____

5. Have you ever had an accident?

   _____

67. Setze die angegebenen Verben in die Lücken:

1. (to be) _____ you ever _____ to Australia?
2. (to drive) _____ you ever _____ a tractor?
3. (to eat) _____ you ever _____ fish and chips?
4. (to win) _____ you ever _____ a race?
5. (to ride) _____ you ever _____ a camel?

68. Wie kannst du auf Englisch fragen?
Diese Wörter helfen dir, die folgenden Fragen zu bilden: *how long?*
kangaroo   to know   Ireland   to break

1. Wie lange bist du schon in Irland?

   _____

2. Wie lange kennst du ihn schon?

   _____

3. Bist du schon einmal in Belfast gewesen?

   _____

4. Hast du schon einmal ein Känguru gesehen?

   _____

5. Hast du dir schon einmal den Arm gebrochen?

   _____

present perfect progressive

I have been writing letters all day.

> Diese Vergangenheitsform verwendest du, um auszudrücken, dass eine **Handlung** oder ein **Vorgang** in der Vergangenheit angefangen hat und **in der Gegenwart noch andauert**.
> Diese Verlaufsform hat oft zusätzliche Erkennungszeichen: Wörter wie *all day* (schon den ganzen Tag), *all morning* (schon den ganzen Morgen), *how long*? (wie lange schon?)

present perfect progressive – bejahte + verneinte Form + Frageform:

Aussagesatz	Frage
I **have** (not) **been waiting**	**Have** I **been waiting**?
you **have** (not) **been waiting**	**Have** you **been waiting**?
he **has** (not) **been waiting**	**Has** he **been waiting**?
she **has** (not) **been waiting**	**Has** she **been waiting**?
it **has** (not) **been waiting**	**Has** it **been waiting**?
we **have** (not) **been waiting**	**Have** we **been waiting**?
you **have** (not) **been waiting**	**Have** you **been waiting**?
they **have** (not) **been waiting**	**Have** they **been waiting**?

- Du brauchst für die bejahte Form *has / have* und *been* sowie die **ing-Form** des Verbs.
- Bei verneinten Sätzen stellst du *not* zwischen *has / have* und *been*.
- Bei Entscheidungsfragen werden einfach nur wieder – wie zum Beispiel im *present progressive* und im *past progressive* – die Plätze getauscht:

Aussagesatz: He **has been waiting** long. = Er **wartet** schon lange.

Fragesatz: **Has** he **been waiting** long? = **Wartet** er schon lange?

Pass hier gut auf: Bei solchen Sätzen steht zwar im Deutschen oft die Gegenwartsform – aber im Englischen brauchst du das **present perfect progressive**!

69. Fülle die Lücken mit einem Verb im **present perfect progressive**.
Diese Verben passen zu den Sätzen: to repair   to smoke   to paint
to rain   to sell   to make   to work   to cry   to write   to look for

1. It _____ for seven days now. There is a lot of water
   in the river.
2. Have you seen my keys? I _____ them all morning.
3. His teeth are very brown. He _____ too many
   cigarettes.
4. I _____ cakes. That's why there is butter on my
   blouse.
5. Tina is very unhappy. She _____ all day.
6. How long _____ you _____
   computers?
7. I _____ my bicycle. That is why my hands are dirty.
8. She _____ to her penfriend for three years now.
9. There is some white paint on his trousers. He
   _____ the walls.
10. Raymond is tired. He _____ very hard all week.

We have been learning English
for two years now.

70. Wie kannst du diese Sätze auf Englisch sagen?
Diese Wörter helfen dir weiter: all morning   to learn   cars
to look for   for two years   to sell   how long   to rain

1. Wie lange lernst du (schon) Englisch?   _____
2. Ich lerne (schon) seit zwei Jahren Englisch.   _____
3. Wie lange regnet es schon?   _____
4. Ich suche dich schon den ganzen Morgen.   _____
5. Wie lange verkaufst du schon Autos?   _____

present perfect simple
oder present perfect progressive

Das *present perfect simple* verwendest du, wenn du
- von etwas berichtest, was zwar in der Vergangenheit angefangen hat, aber noch irgendwie in die Gegenwart hineinreicht.
- über vergangene **Ereignisse** oder **Erlebnisse** berichtest; dich interessiert hier nicht, wann genau es passiert ist, sondern welche Auswirkung es auf die Gegenwart hat.
- zusätzliche Erkennungszeichen: Wörter wie *already, ever, just, never, not yet, yet, how much?, how many?, how many times?*

Das *present perfect progressive* verwendest du, um auszudrücken,
- dass eine **Handlung** oder ein **Vorgang** in der Vergangenheit angefangen hat und **in der Gegenwart noch andauert**.
- zusätzliche Erkennungszeichen: Wörter wie *all day, all morning, how long?*

Es fällt dir sicher jeweils leicht zu entscheiden, ob du eine Form im *present perfect simple* oder im *present perfect progressive* brauchst, wenn du dich an dem Fragebaum orientierst.

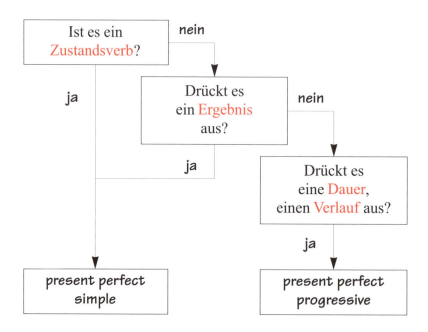

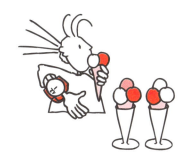

He has just eaten ten ice-creams.

She has been eating ice-cream all morning.

Ergebnis

Du weißt, dass Tom gerade insgesamt zehn Eis **gefuttert** hat. **Du weißt aber nichts über den Verlauf,** denn es wird nicht gesagt, wie lange es gedauert hat.

Verlauf

Du weißt nur, dass diese Aktivität schon den ganzen Morgen **stattgefunden hat. Du weißt aber nicht, ob Lisa nun damit aufhört und auch nichts über das Ergebnis**, denn es wird nicht gesagt, wie viel Eis sie schon gegessen hat.

71. Schreibe jeweils hinter den Satz, ob wichtig ist, dass etwas gerade fertig geworden ist (**Ergebnis**) oder ob wichtig ist, dass jemand etwas schon seit einiger Zeit tut (**Verlauf**).

1. She has read 60 pages. _____
2. She has been reading for three hours. _____
3. I have been painting my bedroom all afternoon. _____
4. I have painted my bedroom. _____
5. They have collected one hundred CDs. _____
6. They have been collecting CDs for a long time. _____

72. Vervollständige die Sätze, indem du die vorangestellten Verben in der richtigen Form einsetzt:

1. (to make) I _____ cakes all morning.
2. (to make) I _____ six cakes.
3. (to walk) He _____ 25 kilometres.
4. (to walk) He _____ for two hours.
5. (to read) She _____ all day.
6. (to read) She _____ two books today.

past oder present perfect

Was ist der Bedeutungsunterschied zwischen *I lost my keys* und *I **have** lost my keys*?

In beiden Sätzen sagst du, dass du deine Schlüssel verloren hast. Jetzt kommt es darauf an, ob du

- sagen willst, dass du sie zwar mal verloren, aber möglicherweise inzwischen wiedergefunden hast – dann sagst du, dass die Handlung (hier: das Verlieren der Schlüssel) abgeschlossen ist. Dann brauchst du einen Satz im *past*.

oder ob

- du sagen willst, dass du sie immer noch nicht finden kannst – dann sagst du, dass die Handlung (hier: das Verlieren der Schlüssel) für die Gegenwart von Bedeutung ist, denn du hast die Schlüssel immer noch nicht gefunden und kannst weder auf- noch zusperren. Dann brauchst du einen Satz im *present perfect*.

Es ist also wichtig, dass du lernst, nach **Signalwörtern** im Satz zu suchen - und zwar nach den richtigen! Manchmal sehen Wörter wie Signalwörter aus, obwohl sie gar keine sind.

Auf Deutsch könntest du zum Beispiel sagen: *Letzten Sommer sind wir in York gewesen* oder: *Wir waren gerade in der Eisdiele*. Vielleicht denkst du jetzt, dass die Signalwörter in diesem Beispiel „sind gewesen" und „waren" sind. Das sind aber gar nicht die wichtigen Wörter. Die Signalwörter sind hier „letzten Sommer" (→ *past*) und „gerade" (→ *present perfect*).

Deshalb: **Suche die richtigen Signalwörter! Die deutschen Zeiten sind NICHT direkt übertragbar!**

I bought a bicycle five years **ago**. (I sold it two years ago).

I have **just** bought a new bicycle.

past: Gute **Signalwörter** sind Wörter wie *yesterday* (gestern), *last week* (letzte Woche), *last year* (letztes Jahr), *five minutes ago* (vor fünf Minuten), *a month ago* (vor einem Monat).

present perfect: Gute **Signalwörter** sind Wörter wie *already* (schon), *ever* (jemals), *just* (gerade), *never* (bisher noch nie), *not yet* (bis jetzt noch nicht), *yet* (bis jetzt).

73. Welche Wörter sind die richtigen **Signalwörter**? Schreibe sie jeweils hinter den Satz:

Signalwörter?

1. He went skiing at the weekend. _____
2. I have already spoken to him. _____
3. He phoned me the day before yesterday. _____
4. Have you ever read "The Wind in the Willows"? _____
5. I saw her two minutes ago. _____
6. We went there last Sunday. _____
7. He has just told me about the accident. _____
8. She left two hours ago. _____
9. That postcard arrived a week ago. _____
10. He hasn't answered yet. _____

74. Finde nun in den deutschen Sätzen die Signalwörter! Ordne sie dann auch noch der Zeit zu, die du im Englischen benötigst, wenn du die Sätze übersetzen willst:

Signalwörter?　*past* oder *present perfect*?

1. Sie hat ihn schon gefragt. _____ _____
2. Sie hat ihn vorgestern gefragt. _____ _____
3. Wir sind vor drei Stunden gekommen. _____ _____
4. Wir sind gerade gekommen. _____ _____
5. Hast du schon mal Schnecken gegessen? _____ _____
6. Vor zwei Minuten ist er noch da gewesen. _____ _____
7. Letzten Mittwoch hat er einen Unfall gehabt. _____ _____
8. Er hat noch nicht angerufen. _____ _____
9. Er hat gestern angerufen. _____ _____
10. Er hat gerade angerufen. _____ _____

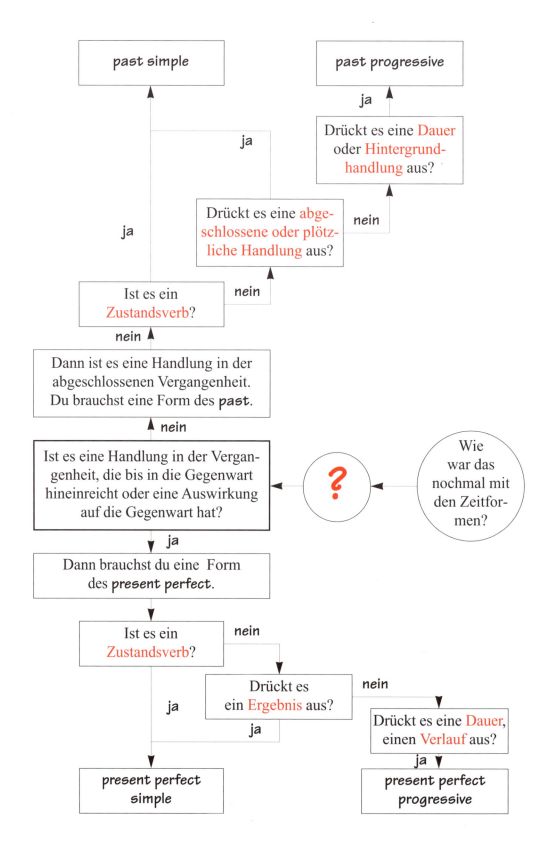

75. Im Radio hörst du einen Bericht über drei Frauen, die auf dem Weg zum Nordpol sind. Eine der Frauen wird über Funk interviewt. Der Interviewer möchte wissen, ob sie den Nordpol schon erreicht haben, was sie erlebt haben und wie es ihnen geht.
Vervollständige die Sätze:

Interviewer: "Hello. Thank you for taking the time to talk to us. _____ you _____ the North Pole yet?" (1. to reach)

Woman: "Yes, we _____ here for about an hour now." (2. to be)

Interviewer: "Congratulations! Well done everybody!"

Woman: "Thank you very much."

Interviewer: "_____ you already _____ up your tents?" (3. to put)

Woman: "Oh yes, we _____ up our tents an hour ago (4. to put). And then we _____ some hot chocolate (5. to have). It is very, very cold at the North Pole, you know."

Interviewer: "_____ you _____ any polar bears on your way to the North Pole?" (6. to see)

Woman: "Yes, we _____ ." (7. *bejahte Kurzantwort*)

Interviewer: "_____ you afraid?" (8. to be)

Woman: "No, we _____ . (9. *verneinte Kurzantwort*) We _____ some nice photographs of them (10. to take). Polar bears are very beautiful animals."

Interviewer: "_____ you _____ any medical problems so far?" (11. to have)

Woman: "No, we _____ any medical problems yet (12. not / to have). We're just very tired and quite cold. But there is another problem. The weather _____ just _____ (13. to change). We're in the middle of a very bad snow storm now."

Interviewer: "I'm sorry to hear that. I hope you are OK. _____ you already _____ to your families?" (14. to speak)

Woman: "Yes, we _____ . (15. *bejahte Kurzantwort*) They are very happy for us."

Zukunft

future simple (= will-future)

Diese Zukunftsform verwendest du, wenn du
- Vermutungen über die Zukunft ausdrücken möchtest,
- Vorhersagen über die Zukunft machen möchtest oder
- spontane Entscheidungen triffst.

Wenn man **Vermutungen** oder **Vorhersagen** machen möchte, dann benutzt man außerdem oft Wörter wie *hoffentlich, vermutlich, wahrscheinlich* usw. Im Englischen ist das genauso.
Häufig findest du als zusätzliche Erkennungszeichen **Signalwörter** wie *hopefully* (hoffentlich), *probably* (wahrscheinlich), usw. oder *to think* (denken), *to hope* (hoffen) usw.

Tom will forget. Lisa won't forget.

future simple – bejahte und verneinte Form:

bejaht		verneint	
Langform	**Kurzform**	**Langform**	**Kurzform**
I **will go**	I**'ll go**	I **will not go**	I **won't go**
you **will go**	you**'ll go**	you **will not go**	you **won't go**
he **will go**	he**'ll go**	he **will not go**	he **won't go**
she **will go**	she**'ll go**	she **will not go**	she **won't go**
it **will go**	it**'ll go**	it **will not go**	it **won't go**
we **will go**	we**'ll go**	we **will not go**	we **won't go**
you **will go**	you**'ll go**	you **will not go**	you **won't go**
they **will go**	they**'ll go**	they **will not go**	they **won't go**

In der **ich-Form** und der **wir-Form** kannst du statt *will* das Wort *shall* benutzen. Dann heißt es in der *bejahten Form I shall* und *we shall*. An der **Abkürzung ändert sich aber nichts**. Die gilt für alle Formen. In der *verneinten Form* kannst du *I shall not* und *we shall not* benutzen. Die **Abkürzung** heißt dann *shan't: I shan't* und *we shan't*.

76. Fülle die Lücken!

Beispiel: (they / be back soon) I hope ... *they will be back soon* ...

1. (it / be all right)
   I think *the voc test will be easy.*
2. (the vocabulary test / be easy)
   I hope _____
3. (he / like the Yorkshire Dales)
   I'm sure *he like the Yorkshire Dales.*
4. (Anna / be at home this afternoon)
   I think *Anna will be at home this afternoon.*
5. (Steven / find his keys)
   I'm sure *Steven will find his keys.*

77. Verneine die folgenden Aussagen.

Beispiel: He will be late. ... *He won't be late.* ...

1. It will break.
   It won't break
2. The weather will be nice tomorrow.
   The weather won't be nice tomorrow.
3. I will see her this evening.
   I won't her see her this evening
4. The test will be difficult.
   The test won't be difficult.
5. We will go out this evening.
   We won't go out this evening

78. Wie kannst du diese Sätze auf Englisch ausdrücken?
Hier stehen Wörter, die dir dabei helfen: *to be at home   to be late   to snow   to win   to rain*

1. Ich glaube, es wird regnen.
   I think _____
2. Ich glaube, es wird schneien.
   _____
3. Ich denke, wir werden morgen zu Hause sein.
   _____
4. Ich denke, sie werden gewinnen.
   _____
5. Ich denke, er wird zu spät kommen.
   _____

Spontane Aktionen

Es gibt Entscheidungen, die man ganz spontan trifft – und da brauchst du dann das *will-future*. Oft sind solche spontanen Aktionen Angebote oder Versprechen, die aus einer Situation heraus entstehen.

Beispiel für eine spontane Entscheidung:
Du warst auf der Toilette im Gasthof, und als du zurückkommst, ist die Bedienung an eurem Tisch und deine Eltern bestellen schon. Du hast keine Zeit zum Überlegen und musst dich ganz schnell entscheiden: *„I'll have an orange juice, please."*

I'll have an orange juice, please.

Beispiel für ein spontanes Angebot:
Du siehst eine Frau, die sich mit ihrer schweren Tasche abmüht. Sie tut dir leid, und du bietest spontan an, ihr zu helfen: *"I'll carry that for you."* Oder: *„Shall I carry that for you?"*

Beispiel für ein spontanes Versprechen:
Dein Freund fragt dich, ob du ein Geheimnis bewahren wirst. Du versprichst spontan: *"I won't tell anybody."*

Beispiel für eine spontane Zustimmung:
Du hast dir ein Paar Jeans gekauft. Deine Freundin sieht sie und zeigt dir, dass die Jeans hinten falsch genäht sind. Du stimmst sofort zu: *"You're right. I'll take them back to the shop."*

79. Fülle die Lücken:

Beispiel: Did you tidy up your room?

Oh no, I forgot. *I'll tidy it up now.*

1. Did you phone Richard?
   Oh no, I forgot. *I'll phone Richard.*
2. Did you write to Charlene?
   Oh no, I forgot. *I'll write to Charlene*
3. Did you ask your mother?
   Oh no, I forgot. *I'll ask my mother.*
4. Did you repair your bike?
   Oh no, I forgot. *I'll repair my bike.*
5. Did you do your homework?
   Oh no, I forgot. *I'll do my homework.*

80. Die Großmutter deines englischen Austauschpartners liegt krank im Bett. Wie kannst du auf Englisch spontan deine Hilfe anbieten?

Beispiel:

I am hungry. (to make some sandwiches) *I'll make you some sandwiches.*

1. Grandmother: I am thirsty. (to make a cup of tea)
   You: *I'll make a cup of tea.*
2. Grandmother: I am cold. (to close the window)
   You: *I'll close the window.*
3. Grandmother: I cannot see very well. (to turn on the light)
   You: *I'll turn on the light.*
4. Grandmother: I don't want to watch TV. (to read a story)
   You: *I'll read a story.*
5. Grandmother: I would like to sleep now. (to turn off the light)
   You: *I'll turn off the light.*

81. Du kommst zu spät ins Café. Die Bedienung ist schon bei den anderen am Tisch und du musst dich ganz schnell entscheiden. Wie kannst du diese Dinge auf Englisch bestellen?

1. ein Glas Milch _____, please.
2. einen Apfelsaft _____, please.
3. eine Tasse Tee _____, please.
4. eine Cola _____, please.
5. eine Tasse Kaffee _____, please.

What will you do this weekend?

I have no plans for the weekend.
What will you do this weekend? Will you go
swimming? Will you go ice-skating? Will there
be an important match this weekend? Will the
shops be open on Saturday afternoon?

Will you go to the
cinema with me
if I ask you?

Will you eat
a lot of dog food?

future simple – Frageform und Kurzantwort:

deutsch	englisch	Kurzantwort
Werde ich …?	**Will I have** …?	**Yes, I will. / No, I won't.**
Wirst du …?	**Will you have** …?	**Yes, you will. / No, you won't.**
Wird er …?	**Will he have** …?	**Yes, he will. / No, he won't.**
Wird sie …?	**Will she have** …?	**Yes, she will. / No, she won't.**
Wird es …?	**Will it have** …?	**Yes, it will. / No, it won't.**
Werden wir …?	**Will we have** …?	**Yes, we will. / No, we won't.**
Werdet ihr …?	**Will you have** …?	**Yes, you will. / No, you won't.**
Werden sie …?	**Will they have** …?	**Yes, they will. / No, they won't.**

In der **ich-Form** und der **wir-Form** kannst du statt *will* das Wort *shall* benutzen. Das Wort *shall* benutzt man oft, wenn man **spontan seine Hilfe anbieten** will.

82. Dein englischer Opa ist mal wieder krank. Wie kannst du ihn auf Englisch danach fragen, wie du ihn aufheitern kannst?

Beispiel: to play the piano *Shall I play the piano for you?*

1. to turn on the TV _____ for you?
2. to sing a song _____ for you?
3. to play cards _____ with you?
4. to bake a cake _____ for you?
5. to cook a nice meal _____ for you?

83. Du fragst einen Freund, was seiner Meinung nach **morgen** passieren wird. Achte gut darauf, dass alle Wörter an der **richtigen Stelle** stehen!

1. Wirst du Aileen morgen sehen?

_____

2. Wird sie den Brief lesen?

_____

3. Wirst du heute nachmittag zu Hause sein?

_____

4. Werden wir einen Englischtest schreiben?

_____

5. Wirst du dich an diese Sätze erinnern?

_____

84. Bilde nun jeweils Fragen mit *will* und einem **Fragewort**.

1. Was wird dein Bruder sagen?

_____

2. Was wird geschehen?

_____

3. Wohin wirst du nach dem Unterricht gehen?

_____

4. Wann wirst du Zeit haben, mir zu helfen?

_____

5. Wann werde ich dich wieder sehen?

_____

to be going to future

I'm going to buy Heather's bike. I'm not going to buy Nigel's bike.

Diese Zukunftsform verwendest du, wenn du ausdrücken möchtest, dass
- du in der Zukunft etwas zu tun beabsichtigst, und dass du das bereits **beschlossen** hast, **bevor** du darüber sprichst,
- etwas **mit Sicherheit** oder **mit großer Wahrscheinlichkeit** eintreten wird, denn es sind bereits Anzeichen dafür vorhanden.

das „going-to-future" – bejahte + verneinte Form

bejaht	verneint
I **am going to**	I **am not going to**
you **are going to**	you **are not going to**
he **is going to**	he **is not going to**
she **is going to**	she **is not going to**
it **is going to**	it **is not going to**
we **are going to**	we **are not going to**
you **are going to**	you **are not going to**
they **are going to**	they **are not going to**

We are going to have a party.

It is going to rain.

Beispiele für den Gebrauch:
„*We are going to have a party.*" (Z. B. dann, wenn man sich schon fest entschlossen hat, eine Feier zu veranstalten und vielleicht sogar schon mitten in den Vorbereitungen steckt.)
„*It is going to rain.*" (Z. B. dann, wenn am Himmel schon dunkle Wolken zu sehen sind, und es also nicht nur eine bloße Vermutung ist, sondern Anzeichen vorhanden sind.)

85. Hast du dir vorgenommen, morgen diese Dinge zu tun? Schreibe wahre Sätze!

Beispiel: (to brush your hair)   *I'm going to brush my hair.*
oder: *I'm **not** going to brush my hair.*

1. (to get up at 5 o'clock) _____
2. (to have a shower) _____
3. (to have a bath) _____
4. (to have breakfast at 6 o'clock) _____
5. (to go to school by car) _____
6. (to do an English test) _____
7. (to have lunch) _____
8. (to have a picnic) _____
9. (to play tennis) _____
10. (to do your homework) _____
11. (to buy a new pair of jeans) _____
12. (to feed the cat) _____
13. (to cook a meal) _____
14. (to wash the dishes) _____

86. Was haben diese Leute für heute abend schon **fest geplant**?

1. Kevin wird seinen Großvater besuchen.
_____

2. Sharon wird fernsehen.
_____

3. Steve wird Fußball spielen.
_____

4. Nicola wird Musik hören.
_____

5. Simon wird mit seinem Hund rausgehen.
_____

6. Emily wird Golf spielen.
_____

7. Chris wird sein Fahrrad reparieren.
_____

8. Ann wird einige Freunde treffen.
_____

9. Raymond wird eine Zeitschrift lesen.
_____

10. Kathryn wird einen Brief schreiben.
_____

What are you going to do tomorrow?

What am I going to have for lunch? And what am I going to have for dinner?

going to future – Frageform und Kurzantwort:

englische Frage	Kurzantwort
am I go**ing to buy** ...?	Yes, I am. / No, I'm not.
are you go**ing to buy** ...?	Yes, you are. / No, you aren't.
is he go**ing to buy** ...?	Yes, he is. / No, he isn't.
is she go**ing to buy** ...?	Yes, she is. / No, she isn't.
is it go**ing to buy** ...?	Yes, it is. / No, it isn't.
are we go**ing to buy** ...?	Yes, we are. / No, we aren't.
are you go**ing to buy** ...?	Yes, you are. / No, you aren't.
are they go**ing to buy** ...?	Yes, they are. / No, they aren't.

Fragen mit Fragewörtern:

What …? (*Was? / Welche?*)	What **are** you go**ing** to do?
Where …? (*Wo?*)	Where **is** your brother go**ing** to be?
Who …? (*Wen?*)	Who **is** he go**ing** to talk to?
How …? (*Wie?*)	How **are** you go**ing** to find it?
When …? (*Wann?*)	When **are** you go**ing** to visit me?
How long …? (*Wie lange?*)	How long **is** he go**ing** to stay here?

87. Du möchtest wissen, was andere vorhaben. Vervollständige die Fragen!
Diese Wörter helfen dir dabei: sing do watch have drive invite
sleep play paint read

1. Are you going to _____ a bath?
2. Is Caroline going to _____ the video?
3. Are you going to _____ "Asterix in Britain"?
4. Is Timothy going to _____ in the living room?
5. Are you going to _____ this room yellow?
6. Is Alex going to _____ his homework?
7. Are you going to _____ cards?
8. Is Daphne going to _____ at the concert?
9. Are you going to _____ Christine to your birthday party?
10. Is Warren going to _____ the other car?

88. Vervollständige die Fragen mit *going-to*-Formen:
1. Wird es nass und windig sein?
   (to be) _____ it _____ wet and windy?
2. Wird es regnen?
   (to rain) _____ it _____ ?
3. Wo wirst du sein?
   (to be) Where _____ you _____ ?
4. Werdet ihr gewinnen?
   (to win) _____ you _____ ?
5. Wirst du zu spät kommen?
   (to be) _____ you _____ late?

89. Einer deiner englischen Freunde plant, sich morgen Mittag mit jeman-
dem in der Stadt zu treffen. Du willst mehr wissen. Wie kannst du ihn
auf Englisch nach seinen Plänen fragen?

1. Wen wirst du treffen?

_____

2. Wo wirst du sie treffen?

_____

3. Wie wirst du dahin kommen?

_____

4. Was wirst du anziehen?

_____

5. Was werdet ihr nach dem Mittagessen machen?

_____

future simple oder to be going to future

Geplante oder vermutete oder spontane Handlung?

- Das *going-to-future* verwendest du für **Pläne**, Absichten oder Vorhaben, die du bereits **beschlossen** hast, **bevor** du darüber sprichst.
- Das **future simple** (= *will-future)* verwendest du für zukünftige Vorgänge, auf die du **keinen Einfluss** hast. Du verwendest es auch für **Vermutungen** oder Vorhersagen über die Zukunft.
- Das *will-future* verwendest du auch für ganz **spontane** Entscheidungen. Oft sind solche spontanen Aktionen z. B. Angebote oder Versprechen, die aus einer Situation heraus entstehen.

Orientiere dich an dem Fragebaum!

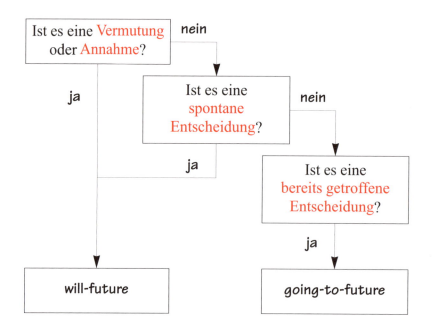

Beispiel für den unterschiedlichen Gebrauch:

- "Oh dear, we haven't got any milk." – "Don't worry. I'll go and get some." (**Angebot erfolgt ganz spontan**, deshalb: *will-future)*
- "Oh dear, we haven't got any milk." – "I know. I'm going to buy some this afternoon." (**Entscheidung war schon getroffen**, deshalb: *going-to-future)*

90. Vervollständige die Sätze mit der richtigen Zeitform!

1. "Did you buy that book for me?" – "Oh, I'm sorry. I forgot. I _____ that now." (to do)

2. "Why have you brought your computer? _____ you _____ tonight?" (to work)

3. "Let's have a party." – "Oh, yes. We _____ all our friends." (to invite)

4. "_____ you _____ this horse? He looks very dangerous to me." (to ride)

5. "Do you know how to use this video recorder?" – "Yes, I _____ you." (to show)

91. Du bist nächste Woche auf Klassenfahrt in Stratford-upon-Avon, aber einer deiner Freunde möchte sich mit dir verabreden. Vervollständige die Sätze!

1. "Do you want to go to the cinema next Thursday?" – "I'm afraid I can't. Our class _____ visit Shakespeare's birthplace next week."

2. "Do you think you _____ enjoy the trip?" – "Yes. But there is one problem: I would like to take some pictures in Stratford-upon-Avon and I haven't got a camera."

3. "No problem. I _____ let you use my camera. I don't need it this week."

4. "Thank you. That is very nice of you. I _____ bring you a nice souvenir and

5. I _____ buy you a new film." – "Thank you!"

92. Du erzählst deinen Freundinnen und Freunden von den Urlaubsplänen deiner Familie. Ihr werdet nach England fahren und direkt an der Küste wohnen. Vervollständige die Sätze!

1. "We _____ spend our summer holidays in Robin Hood's Bay. It is a small village on the Yorkshire coast.

2. We _____ stay for two weeks.

3. I hope the weather _____ be nice.

4. Mum and Dad told me that we _____ visit York Minster. It is a very old cathedral. I hope we _____ also visit Alton Towers. It is a theme park.

5. If we go to Alton Towers I _____ send you a postcard."

Zeitformen in einem Bedingungssatz

Bedingungssätze heißen deshalb **Bedingung**ssätze, weil du damit ausdrücken kannst, was passiert, wenn eine bestimmte **Bedingung** erfüllt oder nicht erfüllt wird. Manchmal werden diese Sätze auch *Wenn-Sätze* genannt. Damit ist das Gleiche gemeint. **Bedingungssätze bestehen aus zwei Teilen**: dem *if*-Satz (also dem *Wenn*-Satz) und dem *Hauptsatz*.

Es gibt verschiedene Arten von Bedingungssätzen. Mit einer Art drückst du aus, dass **wahrscheinlich** etwas geschehen wird, wenn eine bestimmte Bedingung erfüllt wird. Bei solchen Sätzen steht dann **im *if*-Satz das *present simple*** und **im Hauptsatz das *future simple*** (*will-future*).
Es ist egal, ob der *if*-Satz oder der Hauptsatz zuerst steht.

Manchmal steht der ***if*-Satz zuerst**.
Beispiel:

***if*-Satz**	**Hauptsatz**
If I find his address	I will send him a postcard.

schreibe ich ihm eine Postkarte.

Wenn / Falls ich seine Adresse finde,

werde ich ihm eine Postkarte schreiben.

Manchmal steht der **Hauptsatz zuerst**.
Beispiel:

Hauptsatz	***if*-Satz**
I will send him a postcard	if I find his address.

Ich schreibe ihm eine Postkarte,

wenn / falls ich seine Adresse finde.

Ich werde ihm eine Postkarte schreiben,

93. Setze das Verb im *if*-Satz in die richtige Zeitform!

1. If you _____ another ice-cream you will be ill. (to eat)
2. He will ask her if he _____ her. (to see)
3. If I _____ you a horror story will you be frightened? (to tell)
4. We will go to the circus tomorrow if you _____ your homework now. (to do)
5. If she _____ the house will she buy it? (to like)

94. Setze das Verb im **Hauptsatz** in die richtige Zeitform!

1. You _____ there in time if you run fast enough. (to get)
2. If she hears about the accident she _____ very angry. (to be)
3. We _____ without her if she is late again. (to go)
4. If the house catches fire we _____ a problem. (to have)
5. I _____ the zoo if I see a boa constrictor. (to phone)

95. Setze die Verben in die richtige Zeitform! Achte immer gut darauf, ob die Lücke das jeweils einzusetzende Verb im *if*-Satz oder im Hauptsatz erfordert!

1. If it is very far I _____ a taxi. (to take)
2. He will be late if he _____ the train. (to miss)
3. If they speak slowly I _____ them. (to understand)
4. If it _____ dangerous I won't go. (to be)
5. If you _____ the signs you will get there. (to follow)

Unregelmäßige Verben

German infinitive	English infinitive	simple past	past participle
sein	be (am/is/are)	was / were	been
besiegen, schlagen	beat	beat	beaten
werden	become	became	become
anfangen, beginnen	begin	began	begun
wehen, blasen	blow	blew	blown
zerbrechen, kaputtgehen	break	broke	broken
bringen, mitbringen, herbringen	bring	brought	brought
kaufen	buy	bought	bought
fangen, erwischen	catch	caught	caught
wählen, aussuchen	choose	chose	chosen
kommen	come	came	come
tun	do	did	done
ziehen, zeichnen	draw	drew	drawn
trinken	drink	drank	drunk
(Auto) fahren	drive	drove	driven
essen	eat	ate	eaten
fallen	fall	fell	fallen
füttern	feed	fed	fed
fühlen, sich fühlen	feel	felt	felt
finden	find	found	found
fliegen	fly	flew	flown
bekommen, werden	get	got	got
geben	give	gave	given
gehen	go	went	gone
wachsen	grow	grew	grown
haben	have	had	had
hören	hear	heard	heard
verstecken, sich verstecken	hide	hid	hidden
treffen, schlagen	hit	hit	hit
wissen, kennen	know	knew	known
verlassen	leave	left	left
lassen, zulassen	let	let	let
liegen	lie	lay	lain
verlieren	lose	lost	lost

German infinitive	English infinitive	simple past	past participle
machen	make	made	made
bedeuten, meinen	mean	meant	meant
begegnen, treffen	meet	met	met
überholen	overtake	overtook	overtaken
bezahlen	pay	paid	paid
setzen, stellen, legen	put	put	put
lesen	read	read	read
reiten	ride	rode	ridden
läuten	ring	rang	rung
laufen	run	ran	run
sagen	say	said	said
sehen	see	saw	seen
verkaufen	sell	sold	sold
schicken	send	sent	sent
setzen	set	set	set
schütteln	shake	shook	shaken
scheinen	shine	shone	shone
zeigen	show	showed	shown
zumachen, schließen	shut	shut	shut
singen	sing	sang	sung
sitzen	sit	sat	sat
schlafen	sleep	slept	slept
sprechen	speak	spoke	spoken
buchstabieren	spell	spelt	spelt
(Geld) ausgeben, (Urlaub) verbringen	spend	spent	spent
stehen	stand	stood	stood
schwimmen	swim	swam	swum
nehmen, mitnehmen, wegbringen	take	took	taken
unterrichten, lehren	teach	taught	taught
erzählen, berichten, sagen	tell	told	told
meinen, denken	think	thought	thought
werfen	throw	threw	thrown
begreifen, verstehen	understand	understood	understood
anhaben, (Kleidung) tragen	wear	wore	worn
siegen, gewinnen	win	won	won
schreiben	write	wrote	written

Lösungen

1. 1. My father is a baker. 2. Jupiter is a planet. 3. The pupils are noisy. 4. Apples and bananas are types of fruit. 5. York and London are cities in England.

2. 1. is 2. are 3. am 4. are 5. are

3. 1. We are hungry. 2. I am tall. 3. They are boring. 4. That is fantastic! 5. You are tired.

4. 1. aren't 2. isn't 3. aren't 4. 'm not 5. aren't

5. 1. isn't 2. 'm not 3. isn't 4. aren't 5. isn't

6. 1. These shoes aren't expensive. 2. Lawrence isn't short. 3. We aren't happy. 4. He isn't untidy. 5. I'm not thirsty.

7. 1. Is Garfield a dog? No, he isn't. 2. Am I late? Yes, you are. 3. Are you the President of the United States of America? No, I'm not. 4. Is this your bicycle? Yes, it is. 5. Are they at home? No, they aren't.

8. 1. Are we ready? 2. Is she a doctor? 3. Are the children in bed? 4. Are you angry? 5. Are you crazy?

9. 1. Where is that? 2. Who are they? 3. What is wrong? 4. Why are you so quiet? 5. What is your name?

10. 1. is wearing 2. am waiting 3. is playing 4. am trying 5. are going

11. 1. The cat is climbing a tree. 2. Listen! The dogs are barking. 3. Moritz is visiting a friend. 4. We are having breakfast. 5. The plane is landing. 6. It is raining. 7. Look! Claudia is wearing her new trousers. 8. Listen! Raymond is playing the trumpet. 9. Dad is reading the newspaper. 10. Mum is listening to music.

12. 1. writing 2. swimming 3. listening 4. running 5. driving 6. wearing 7. helping 8. getting 9. looking 10. having 11. opening 12. stopping

13. 1. isn't 2. aren't 3. isn't 4. 'm not 5. aren't

14. 1. 'm not eating 2. aren't having 3. isn't snowing 4. aren't writing
5. isn't ringing

15. 1. The children aren't playing in the garden. 2. I'm not wearing a hat.
3. You aren't listening to me! 4. Christopher isn't doing his homework.
5. I'm not riding an elephant.

16. 1. Are they ...? Yes, they are. 2. Is he ...? No, he is not. / No, he isn't.
3. Are you ...? Yes, I am. 4. Are we ...? No, we are not. / No, we aren't.
5. Is she ...? Yes, she is.

17. 1. Are you having lunch? 2. Are you having a shower? 3. Is she
repairing her bike? 4. Are you making tea? 5. Are you going to the zoo?

18. 1. Where are you going? 2. What are they saying? 3. Who is tidying
up? 4. Why are you crying? 5. When are you leaving?

19. 1. read 2. open 3. likes 4. work 5. speaks

20. 1. The phone often rings. 2. We always work from 9 to 5. 3. She never
gets up before 6 o'clock. 4. He usually does his homework.
5. I sometimes play the guitar.

21. 1. We usually get up at 7 o'clock. 2. He always does his homework.
3. I sometimes go to the cinema. 4. They often take their dog for a
walk. 5. You never listen to me!

22. 1. he goes 2. she buys 3. he wishes 4. she misses 5. it does 6. he finishes
7. she relaxcs 8. he carries 9. she catches 10. she enjoys 11. he tidies
12. she brushes.

23. 1. don't 2. doesn't 3. don't 4. doesn't 5. don't.

24. 1. don't eat 2. doesn't play 3. doesn't like 4. don't like 5. doesn't have

25. 1. I don't have a car. 2. We don't work on Saturdays. 3. Sharon doesn't
play the piano. 4. Jonathan doesn't go dancing. 5. They don't speak
English.

26. 1. Do they ...? Yes, they do. 2. Does he ...? No, he does not. / No, he
doesn't. 3. Do you know ...? Yes, I do. 4. Do we have ...? No, we do
not. / No, we don't. 5. Does she have ...? Yes, she does.

27. 1. Do you often go on holiday? 2. Do you have a hamster? 3. Do they play football? 4. Do they speak German? 5. Do you like chocolate?

28. 1. Where do you live? 2. What does that mean? / What does it mean? 3. What does it look like? / How does it look? 4. How often do you go to the cinema? 5. When do you get up?

29. 1. "What do you think of this new CD?" – "It's great!" 2. "What are you thinking about?" – "I'm thinking about the test tomorrow." 3. "What do you think of the new teacher?" – "He is boring!" 4. What are you thinking about?" – "I'm thinking about my mum. She's in hospital."

30. 1. Yes, I am having a lot of fun. 2. I have a new car. 3. I am having a shower. 4. No, I am having breakfast.

31. 1. Now I understand. 2. Now I remember. 3. Now I know. 4. What is she thinking about?

32. 1. What do you think of it? 2. What are you thinking about? 3. What do you do? 4. What are you doing?

33. 1. am coming 2. speaks, don't understand 3. drinks, is drinking 4. has 5. is having 6. Do [you] love 7. goes 8. am going 9. learn 10. is learning 11. doesn't rain 12. isn't raining

34. 1. was 2. was 3. were 4. was 5. were

35. 1. These shoes were expensive. 2. Last year we were in York. 3. Last week I was in Birmingham. 4. She was happy. 5. It was boring.

36. 1. You were at school. 2. I was ill. I was in bed. 3. We were in hospital. 4. He was at the hotel. 5. They were at the museum.

37. 1. wasn't 2. wasn't 3. weren't 4. wasn't 5. wasn't

38. 1. Tom and Lisa weren't (*oder:* were not) at the cinema. 2. Lisa wasn't (*oder:* was not) at work. 3. Tom wasn't (*oder:* was not) at home. 4. Tom and Lisa weren't (*oder:* were not) at the restaurant. 5. They were at a party!

39. 1. The food wasn't (*oder:* was not) cheap enough. 2. The water in the lake wasn't (*oder:* was not) warm enough. 3. The rooms weren't (*oder:* were not) clean enough. 4. The pool wasn't (*oder:* was not) big enough. 5. The weather wasn't (*oder:* was not) nice enough.

40. 1. Was it nice? Yes, it was. 2. Were the people friendly? Yes, they were. 3. Were there any dogs? Yes, there were. 4. Were you afraid? No, I wasn't / No, I was not. 5. Were you homesick? No, I wasn't / No, I was not.

41. 1. Were they interesting? 2. Was it cold / Were you cold? 3. Were you tired? 4. Was it hot? 5. Were they difficult?

42. 1. Where were you? 2. What was the problem? 3. Why were you so angry? 4. When was that? 5. Who was at the cinema yesterday?

43. 1. I wasn't well yesterday so I stayed in bed. 2. The film started at 8 o'clock and it finished at 10 o'clock. 3. The dog barked at the cat. 4. Princess Diana lived from 1961 to 1997. 5. The accident happened last night. 6. The Robsons don't live here anymore. They moved to Dublin last summer. 7. They wanted to go for a walk but then it started to rain. 8. She parked the car outside the restaurant. 9. Last night we watched television. The film wasn't very good. 10. The ambulance men saved the man's life. 11. Vivienne was late but her friends waited for her. 12. We enjoyed our holiday in Ireland. The people were very friendly. 13. There was no bus so they walked home. 14. He tried to answer the question but it was too difficult.

44. 1. ... this Saturday we played golf. 2. ... this week we walked to school. 3. ... yesterday we helped in the garden. 4. ... this week it rained every day. 5. ... yesterday he shouted at me.

45. 1. drank 2. went 3. knew 4. made 5. spent 6. thought 7. told 8. forgot 9. won 10. wrote

46. 1. found 2. ran 3. fell 4. hurt 5. heard 6. paid 7. flew 8. bought 9. wore 10. understood

47. 1. The red car didn't overtake the blue one. 2. He didn't feed the animals. 3. You didn't eat meat. 4. They didn't buy a magazine. 5. She didn't swim to the other side of the lake. 6. He didn't write me a letter yesterday. 7. They didn't forget to buy a present. 8. She didn't sell her bicycle to a friend. 9. They didn't spend a lot of money.

10. Mrs. Williams didn't teach Spanish. 11. He didn't draw a nice picture. 12. We didn't go to a restaurant.

48. Hier kommt es darauf an, ob du einen **bejahten** oder einen **verneinten** Satz bilden wolltest. Es sind beide Lösungen angegeben – such dir die heraus, die zu deinem Satz passt:
1. I got up before 8 o'clock. / I didn't get up before 8 o'clock. 2. I went to school. / I didn't go to school. 3. I spoke English. / I didn't speak English. 4. I did my homework. / I didn't do my homework. 5. I baked a cake. / I didn't bake a cake. 6. I did the shopping. / I didn't do the shopping. 7. I played football. / I didn't play football. 8. I listened to music. / I didn't listen to music. 9. I had a bath. / I didn't have a bath. 10. I went to the cinema. / I didn't go to the cinema.

49. Für die Fragen, die du bejahen möchtest, verwendest du: *Yes, I did.* Für die, die du verneinen möchtest, verwendest du in der Langform: *No, I did not,* oder in der Kurzform: *No, I didn't.*

50. 1. Did you hear a strange noise last night? 2. Did you see a ghost? 3. Did you run away? 4. Did you hide under the bed? 5. Did you stay there all night?

51. 1. Which magazine did you buy? 2. Why did they leave the room? 3. When did you phone me? 4. How long did it take? 5. How much did you spend? / How much money did you spend? 6. What time did he arrive? 7. Who did you meet? 8. Which one did she choose? 9. Where did you go? 10. What did they have for breakfast?

52. 1. were doing 2. were playing 3. was feeding 4. was reading 5. were having 6. was taking 7. was doing 8. were preparing 9. was working 10. was watching 11. was washing 12. was writing 13. was looking for 14. was teaching 15. was talking 16. were driving 17. were playing 18. were repairing 19. was listening 20. was taking part in
WER WAR'S? Mr. Carmichael sagt wohl nicht die Wahrheit, denn Carlisles und Deans sagen übereinstimmend, dass sie miteinander Karten gespielt haben!

53. 1. Maggie wasn't (*oder:* was not) practising the clarinet. 2. Andrew wasn't (*oder:* was not) baking a cake. 3. Isobel and Richard weren't (*oder:* were not) driving home. 4. Darren wasn't (*oder:* was not) playing football. 5. Shireen wasn't (*oder:* was not) teaching French.

54. 1. Elaine wasn't (*oder:* was not) cleaning the board. 2. Colin and Alan weren't (*oder:* were not) reading the text. 3. Perry and Ross weren't (*oder:* were not) doing their project work. 4. David wasn't (*oder:* was not) listening to his teacher. 5. Lindsay and Joanne weren't (*oder:* were not) using their maps.

55. 1. Sharon wasn't (*oder:* was not) riding a bicycle, she was riding a horse. 2. Nigel wasn't (*oder:* was not) playing hockey, he was playing rugby. 3. Judy wasn't (*oder:* was not) reading Shakespeare, she was reading comics.

56. 1. Were [they] playing 2. Was [she] working 3. Was [the sun] shining 4. Was [he still] sleeping 5. Were [you] having

57. Für die Fragen, die du bejahen möchtest, verwendest du: *Yes, I was.* Für die, die du verneinen möchtest, verwendest du in der Langform: *No, I was not.* Oder in der Kurzform: *No, I wasn't.*

58. 1. Were you watching TV / television? 2. Were you reading a book? 3. Were you repairing your bike / your bicycle? 4. Were you baking a cake? 5. Were you having a bath?

59. 1. *Hier geschieht alles nacheinander* → **past simple:** got, washed, put, had; went; worked; had, had; went. 2. *Hier geschehen alle Aktivitäten gleichzeitig* → **past progressive:** was listening, was playing; was playing, was playing; was washing, was preparing; was reading.

60. 1. was having, rang 2. went, was shining 3. were sitting, started 4. was walking, saw 5. was driving, had

61. 1. We have been very busy. 2. He has written to me. 3. We have had a wonderful holiday. 4. I have already drunk five cups of tea. 5. He has just gone out. 6. She has already phoned him. 7. I have just made some coffee. 8. We have already asked you three times. 9. She has just repaired her bicycle. 10. They have never been to Japan.

62. 1. has done 2. has washed 3. has dried 4. have washed 5. has phoned 6. has watered 7. has bought 8. has fed 9. have taken 10. have brought

63. 1. I haven't (*oder:* have not) tried to learn English. 2. Helen hasn't (*oder:* has not) gone home. 3. We haven't (*oder:* have not) found the answer. 4. I haven't (*oder:* have not) finished this exercise.

5. Alan hasn't (*oder:* has not) been to the cinema.

64. 1. for 2. since 3. since 4. for 5. for 6. since 7. for 8. since 9. since 10. for

65. 1. Geoffrey hasn't (*oder:* has not) found his keys yet. 2. They haven't (*oder:* have not) cleaned the house for years. 3. Perry hasn't (*oder:* has not) read the book yet. 4. Jason hasn't (*oder:* has not) seen Kylie for two weeks. 5. Francis hasn't (*oder:* has not) fed the cat yet.

66. Für die Fragen, die du bejahen möchtest, verwendest du: *Yes, I have.* Für die, die du verneinen möchtest, verwendest du in der Langform: *No, I have not.* Oder in der Kurzform: *No, I haven't.*

67. 1. Have [you ever] been 2. Have [you ever] driven 3. Have [you ever] eaten 4. Have [you ever] won 5. Have [you ever] ridden

68. 1. How long have you been in Ireland? 2. How long have you known him? 3. Have you ever been to Belfast? 4. Have you ever seen a kangaroo? 5. Have you ever broken your arm?

69. 1. has been raining 2. have been looking for 3. has been smoking 4. have been making 5. has been crying 6. have [you] been selling 7. have been repairing 8. has been writing 9. has been painting 10. has been working

70. 1. How long have you been learning English? 2. I have been learning English for two years. 3. How long has it been raining? 4. I have been looking for you all morning. 5. How long have you been selling cars?

71. 1. Ergebnis 2. Verlauf 3. Verlauf 4. Ergebnis 5. Ergebnis 6. Verlauf

72. 1. have been making 2. have made 3. has walked 4. has been walking 5. has been reading 6. has read

73. 1. at the weekend 2. already 3. the day before yesterday 4. ever 5. two minutes ago 6. last Sunday 7. just 8. two hours ago 9. a week ago 10. yet

74. 1. schon, *present perfect* 2. vorgestern, *past* 3. vor drei Stunden, *past* 4. gerade, *present perfect* 5. schon mal, *present perfect* 6. vor zwei Minuten, *past* 7. Letzten Mittwoch, *past* 8. noch nicht, *present perfect*

9. gestern, *past* 10. gerade, *present perfect*

75. 1. Have ... reached 2. have been 3. Have ... put 4. put 5. had 6. Did ... see 7. did 8. Were 9. weren't / were not 10. took 11. Have ... had 12. haven't had / have not had 13. has ... changed 14. have ... spoken 15. have

76. 1. I think it will be all right. 2. I hope the vocabulary test will be easy. 3. I'm sure he will like the Yorkshire Dales. 4. I think Anna will be at home this afternoon. 5. I'm sure Steven will find his keys.

77. 1. It won't break. 2. The weather won't be nice tomorrow. 3. I won't see her this evening. 4. The test won't be difficult. 5. We won't go out this evening.

78. 1. I think it'll rain. 2. I think it'll snow. 3. I think we'll be at home tomorrow. 4. I think they'll win. 5. I think he'll be late.

79. 1. I'll phone him now. 2. I'll write to her now. 3. I'll ask her now. 4. I'll repair it now. 5. I'll do it now.

80. 1. I'll make you a cup of tea. 2. I'll close the window. 3. I'll turn on the light. 4. I'll read you a story. 5. I'll turn off the light.

81. 1. I'll have a glass of milk, please. 2. I'll have an apple juice, please. 3. I'll have a cup of tea, please. 4. I'll have a coke, please. 5. I'll have a cup of coffee, please.

82. 1. Shall I turn on the TV for you? 2. Shall I sing a song for you? 3. Shall I play cards with you? 4. Shall I bake a cake for you? 5. Shall I cook a nice meal for you?

83. 1. Will you see Aileen tomorrow? 2. Will she read the letter? 3. Will you be at home this afternoon? 4. Will we have an English test? 5. Will you remember these sentences?

84. 1. What will your brother say? 2. What will happen? 3. Where will you go after the lesson? 4. When will you have time to help me? 5. When will I see you again?

85. Ob deine Antwort ein *not* enthält oder nicht, hängt davon ab, ob du ei-

nen bejahten oder einen verneinten Satz machen wolltest.
1. I'm (not) going to get up at 5 o'clock. 2. I'm (not) going to have a shower. 3. I'm (not) going to have a bath. 4. I'm (not) going to have breakfast at 6 o'clock. 5. I'm (not) going to go to school by car. 6. I'm (not) going to do an English test. 7. I'm (not) going to have lunch. 8. I'm (not) going to have a picnic. 9. I'm (not) going to play tennis. 10. I'm (not) going to do my homework. 11. I'm (not) going to buy a new pair of jeans. 12. I'm (not) going to feed the cat. 13. I'm (not) going to cook a meal. 14. I'm (not) going to wash the dishes.

86. 1. Kevin is going to visit his grandfather. 2. Sharon is going to watch TV. 3. Steve is going to play football. 4. Nicola is going to listen to music. 5. Simon is going to take his dog for a walk. 6. Emily is going to play golf. 7. Chris is going to repair his bicycle (*oder:* his bike). 8. Ann is going to meet some friends. 9. Raymond is going to read a magazine. 10. Kathryn is going to write a letter.

87. 1. have 2. watch 3. read 4. sleep 5. paint 6. do 7. play 8. sing 9. invite 10. drive

88. 1. Is it going to be wet and windy? 2. Is it going to rain? 3. Where are you going to be? 4. Are you going to win? 5. Are you going to be late?

89. 1. Who are you going to meet? 2. Where are you going to meet her? 3. How are you going to get there? 4. What are you going to wear? 5. What are you going to do after lunch?

90. 1. 'll do / will do / shall do 2. Are [you] going to work 3. 'll invite / will invite / shall invite 4. Are [you] going to ride 5. 'll show / will show / shall show

91. 1. is going to 2. 'll / will 3. 'll / will / shall 4. 'll / will / shall 5. 'll / will / shall

92. 1. are going to 2. are going to 3. 'll / will 4. are going to, 'll / will / shall 5. 'll / will / shall

93. 1. eat 2. sees 3. tell 4. do 5. likes

94. 1. will get 2. will be 3. will go 4. will have 5. will phone

95. 1. will take 2. misses 3. will understand 4. is 5. follow

Das Wichtigste auf einen Blick

Hier siehst du nochmal ganz genau, was du im Englischen mit den Zeiten ausdrücken oder betonen kannst:

Gegenwart

PRESENT SIMPLE:

- dass etwas **regelmäßig** passiert oder dass jemand etwas **gewohnheitsmäßig** oder **nie** tut
- zusätzliche Erkennungszeichen: Wörter wie *always, usually, often, sometimes, never, every day, every year*

PRESENT PROGRESSIVE:

- dass **gerade** etwas passiert oder dass jemand **gerade dabei ist, etwas zu tun**
- zusätzliche Erkennungszeichen: Wörter wie *at the moment, now*; manchmal auch: *today, this morning, this week*

Vergangenheit

PAST SIMPLE:

- **wann** jemand etwas getan hat oder wann etwas geschehen ist
- dass die Ereignisse oder Handlungen **abgeschlossen** oder **vorbei** sind
- dass mehrere Handlungen in der Vergangenheit **nacheinander** folgen
- zusätzliche Erkennungszeichen: Wörter wie *yesterday, last week, last month, last year, five minutes ago, a year ago*

PAST PROGRESSIVE:

- die **Entwicklung** und den Verlauf von etwas, das **eine Zeit lang andauerte**
- dass mehrere Handlungen **gleichzeitig** ausgeführt wurden
- die Beschreibung von Hintergrundhandlungen oder Begleitumständen

PRESENT PERFECT SIMPLE:

- was zwar **in der Vergangenheit angefangen hat**, aber noch irgendwie **in die Gegenwart hineinreicht**
- dass du vor allem Interesse daran hast, welche **Auswirkung es auf die Gegenwart** hat
- zusätzliche Erkennungszeichen: Wörter wie *already* (schon), *ever* (jemals), *just* (gerade), *never* (bisher noch nie), *not yet* (bis jetzt noch nicht), *yet* (bis jetzt), *how much?* (wie viel?), *how many?* (wie viele?), *how many times?* (wie oft?)

PRESENT PERFECT PROGRESSIVE:

- was zwar in der Vergangenheit angefangen hat, aber noch andauert
- zusätzliche Erkennungszeichen: Wörter wie *all day* (schon den ganzen Tag lang), *all morning* (schon den ganzen Morgen lang), *how long?* (wie lange schon?)

Zukunft

GOING-TO-FUTURE:

- **Pläne**, Absichten oder Vorhaben, die du bereits **beschlossen** hast, **bevor** du darüber sprichst.

FUTURE SIMPLE (= WILL-FUTURE):
- zukünftige Vorgänge, auf die du **keinen Einfluss** hast
- **Vermutungen** oder Vorhersagen über die **Zukunft**
- ganz **spontane** Entscheidungen, z. B.: Angebote oder Versprechen, die aus einer Situation heraus entstehen

Zeitformen in einem Bedingungssatz

BEDINGUNGSSÄTZE (TYP PRÄSENS-FUTUR):

- dass **wahrscheinlich** etwas geschehen wird, wenn eine bestimmte Bedingung erfüllt wird
- im *if*-**Satz** steht **das** *present simple* und im **Hauptsatz das** *future simple* (= *will-future*)

Verlaufsformen

Achtung: Nicht alle Verben haben eine „ing-Form"!

I know!

Die wichtigsten Verben, die üblicherweise **nicht in der Verlaufsform** verwendet werden, sind Verben, die ausdrücken, was jemand ...:

(1) ist oder besitzt	Beispiele: *to be, to have* (besitzen)
(2) weiß, versteht, denkt	Beispiele: *to mean, to remember, to know, to understand*
(3) mag, wünscht	Beispiele: *to like, to love, to hate, to want, to need*
(4) mit den Sinnen wahrnimmt	Beispiele: *to hear, to see*